maranGraphics™ Learn at First Sight™

Excel 5 for Windows™ Expanded

D0573588

maranGraphics' Development Group

**Published in the United States
by Prentice Hall, Inc.**

Telephone: 1-800-223-1360
Fax: 1-800-445-6991

**Distributed in Canada
by Prentice Hall Canada**

Telephone: 1-800-567-3800
Fax: 416-299-2529

Corporate Sales (Canada)

Telephone: 1-800-469-6616, ext. 206
Fax: 905-890-9434

**Distributed Internationally
by Simon & Schuster**

Telephone: 201-767-4990
Fax: 201-767-5625

Single Copy Purchases (US)

Telephone: 1-800-947-7700
Fax: 515-284-2607

maranGraphics™ ***Learn at First Sight***™
Excel 5 for Windows™ ***Expanded***

Trademark Acknowledgments

maranGraphics Inc. has attempted to include trademark information for products, services and companies referred to in this guide. Although maranGraphics Inc. has made reasonable efforts in gathering this information, it cannot guarantee its accuracy.

Microsoft, MS, MS-DOS, and XL design (the Microsoft Excel logo) are registered trademarks and AutoSum, Windows, and Windows NT are trademarks of Microsoft Corporation in the United States of America and other countries.

Published by Prentice Hall, Inc.
A Paramount Publishing Company
Englewood Cliffs, New Jersey 07632

Library of Congress Cataloging-in-Publication Data

MaranGraphics Learn at first sight Excel 5 for Windows expanded /
    MaranGraphics' Development Group.
        p.   cm.
    ISBN 0-13-310723-X
    1. Microsoft Excel for Windows.   2. Business--Computer programs.
3. Electronic Spreadsheets.   I. MaranGraphics Development Group.
HF5548.4.M523M273 1994
005.369--dc20   94-17894
                                                            CIP

©1994
maranGraphics, Inc.

The animated characters are the copyright of maranGraphics, Inc.

Learn at First Sight™

EXCEL 5

FOR WINDOWS™

EXPANDED EDITION

maranGraphics™

Credits

Author:

Ruth Maran

Copy Developer:

Kelleigh Wing

Technical Consultant:

Wendi Blouin Ewbank

Designers:

David de Haas

Lance Pilon

Layout Artist:

David de Haas

Illustrator:

Dave Ross

Illustration Revisor:

Carol Walthers

Screen Artists:

David de Haas

Dave Ross

Christie Van Duin

Carol Walthers

Editors:

Judy Maran

Kelleigh Wing

Post Production:

Robert Maran

Acknowledgments

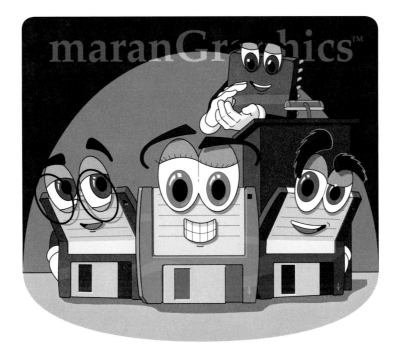

Deepest thanks to Wendi B. Ewbank for her dedication and support in ensuring the technical accuracy of this book.

Thanks to Terry Blanchard of Microsoft Canada Inc. for his support and consultation.

Thanks also to Saverio C. Tropiano for his assistance and expert advice.

Thanks to the dedicated staff of maranGraphics including, David de Haas, Peters Ezers, David Hendricks, Jill Maran, Judy Maran, Maxine Maran, Robert Maran, Dave Ross, Christie Van Duin, Carol Walthers and Kelleigh Wing.

Finally, to Richard Maran who originated the easy-to-use graphic format of this guide. Thank you for your inspiration and guidance.

TABLE OF CONTENTS

INTRODUCTION TO EXCEL

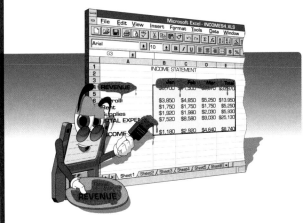

Change Your Screen Display

Using Multiple Worksheets

Using Multiple Workbooks

Charting Data

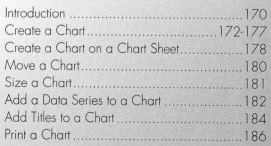

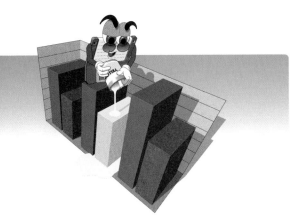

Overview

GETTING STARTED

◆ In this chapter, you will learn the basic skills needed to use Excel.

INTRODUCTION

Microsoft® Excel 5.0 for Windows™ is a spreadsheet program that will save you time and increase the accuracy of your calculations.

ASSUMPTIONS

◆ You have installed the Excel 5.0 for Windows program on your hard drive.

◆ You are using a mouse with Excel 5.0 for Windows.

HOW YOU CAN USE EXCEL

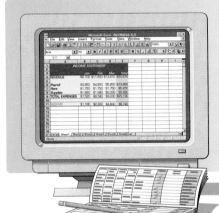

PERSONAL FINANCES

Excel helps you keep track of your mortgage, balance your checkbook, create a personal budget, compare investments and prepare your taxes.

FINANCIAL REPORTS

Businesses of all sizes use spreadsheets to analyze financial information. Excel's formatting and charting features help you present your results in professional looking documents.

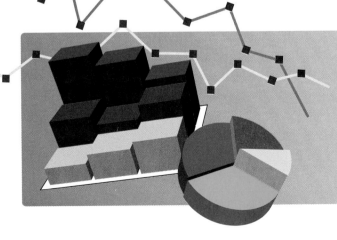

CHARTS

Excel makes it easy to create charts from your spreadsheet data. Charts let you visually illustrate the relationship between different items.

USING
THE MOUSE

The mouse is a hand-held device that lets you quickly select commands and perform tasks.

USING THE MOUSE

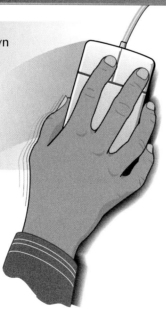

◆ Hold the mouse as shown in the diagram. Use your thumb and two rightmost fingers to guide the mouse while your two remaining fingers press the mouse buttons.

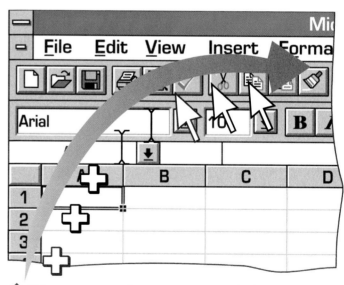

◆ When you move the mouse on your desk, the mouse pointer (⇩ , I or ▨) on your screen moves in the same direction. The mouse pointer changes shape depending on its location on your screen and the action you are performing.

PARTS OF THE MOUSE

◆ The mouse has a left and right button. You can use these buttons to:

- open menus
- select commands
- choose options

Note: You will use the left button most of the time.

◆ Under the mouse is a ball that senses movement. To ensure smooth motion of the mouse, you should occasionally remove and clean this ball.

MOUSE TERMS

CLICK
Quickly press and release the left mouse button once.

DOUBLE-CLICK
Quickly press and release the left mouse button twice.

DRAG
When the mouse pointer (✛, I or ↖) is over an object on your screen, press and hold down the left mouse button and then move the mouse.

START EXCEL

When you start Excel, a blank worksheet appears. You can enter data into this worksheet.

START EXCEL

C:\> win _

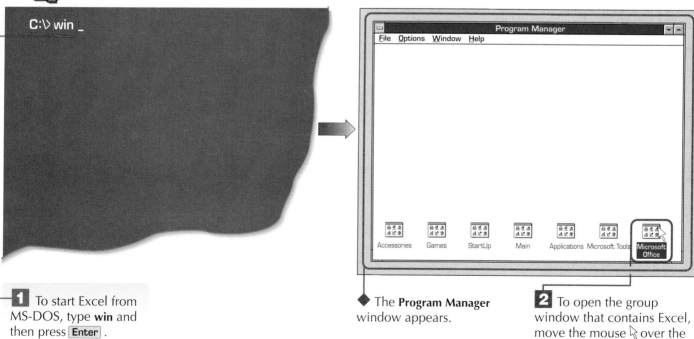

1 To start Excel from MS-DOS, type **win** and then press **Enter**.

◆ The **Program Manager** window appears.

2 To open the group window that contains Excel, move the mouse ⇘ over the icon (example: **Microsoft Office**) and then quickly press the left button twice.

| Getting Started | Save and Open Your Workbooks | Edit Your Worksheets | Using Formulas and Functions | Working with Rows and Columns | Format Your Worksheets | Smart Formatting | Print Your Worksheets |

- Introduction
- Using the Mouse
- **Start Excel**
- Excel Basics
- Enter Data
- Select Cells

- Using AutoFill
- Using the Menus
- The Toolbars
- Move Through a Worksheet
- Getting Help

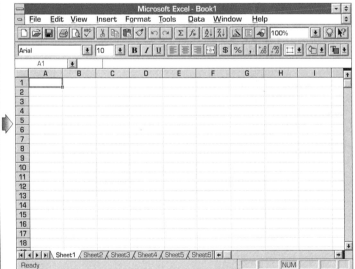

Tip

*The worksheet displayed on your screen is part of a workbook. A workbook is like a three-ring binder that contains several sheets of paper. The name of the workbook is displayed at the top of your screen (example: **Book1**).*

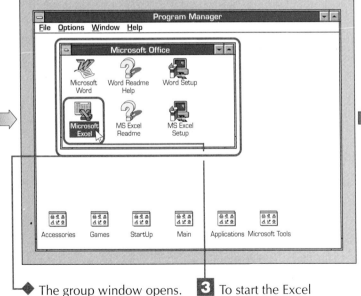

◆ The group window opens.

3 To start the Excel application, move the mouse over **Microsoft Excel** and then quickly press the left button twice.

◆ The **Microsoft Excel** window appears, displaying a blank worksheet.

7

EXCEL BASICS

A worksheet consists of columns, rows and cells.

COLUMNS, ROWS AND CELLS

◆ Column

A column is a vertical line of boxes. Excel labels the columns in a worksheet (example: **F**).

◆ Row

A row is a horizontal line of boxes. Excel numbers the rows in a worksheet (example: **8**).

◆ Cell

A cell is the area where a row and column intersect (example: **F8**).

| Getting Started | Save and Open Your Workbooks | Edit Your Worksheets | Using Formulas and Functions | Working with Rows and Columns | Format Your Worksheets | Smart Formatting | Print Your Worksheets |

- Introduction
- Using the Mouse
- Start Excel
- **Excel Basics**
- Enter Data
- Select Cells

- Using AutoFill
- Using the Menus
- The Toolbars
- Move Through a Worksheet
- Getting Help

THE ACTIVE CELL

ACTIVE CELL

◆ The active cell displays a thick border. You can only enter data into the active cell.

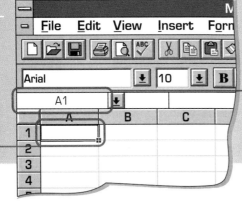

CELL REFERENCE

◆ A cell reference defines the location of each cell. It consists of a column letter followed by a row number (example: **A1**).

The cell reference of the active cell appears at the top of your worksheet.

CHANGE THE ACTIVE CELL

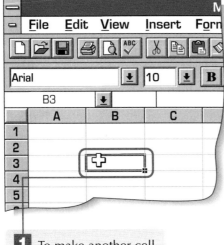

1 To make another cell on your screen the active cell, move the mouse over the cell and then press the left button.

◆ The cell now displays a thick border.

USING THE KEYBOARD

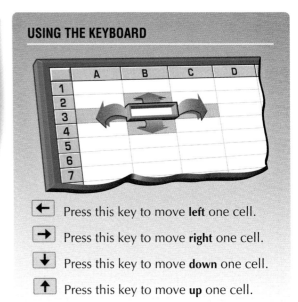

← Press this key to move **left** one cell.

→ Press this key to move **right** one cell.

↓ Press this key to move **down** one cell.

↑ Press this key to move **up** one cell.

9

ENTER DATA

You enter data into the cells of your worksheet using your keyboard.

ENTER DATA

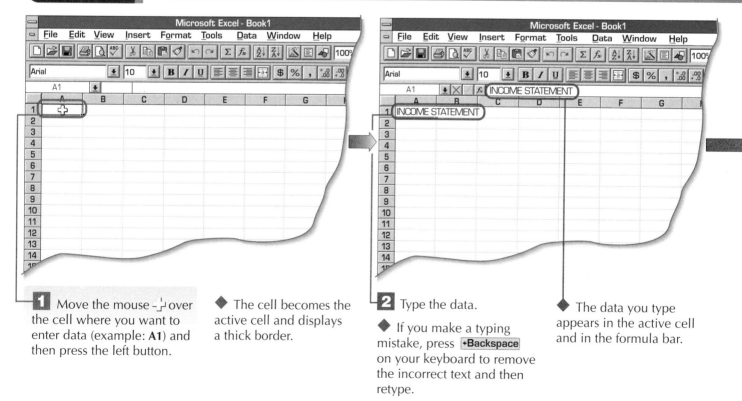

1 Move the mouse ⊕ over the cell where you want to enter data (example: **A1**) and then press the left button.

◆ The cell becomes the active cell and displays a thick border.

2 Type the data.

◆ If you make a typing mistake, press **⬅Backspace** on your keyboard to remove the incorrect text and then retype.

◆ The data you type appears in the active cell and in the formula bar.

10

- Introduction
- Using the Mouse
- Start Excel
- Excel Basics
- **Enter Data**
- Select Cells

- Using AutoFill
- Using the Menus
- The Toolbars
- Move Through a Worksheet
- Getting Help

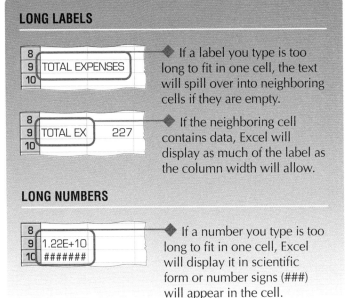

Tip

◆ You can press Num Lock to switch the keys on the right side of your keyboard between number and movement keys.

◆ When **NUM** is visible at the bottom of your screen, you can use the number keys 0 through 9 to quickly enter numbers.

◆ When **NUM** is not visible at the bottom of your screen, you can use the movement keys to move through your worksheet.

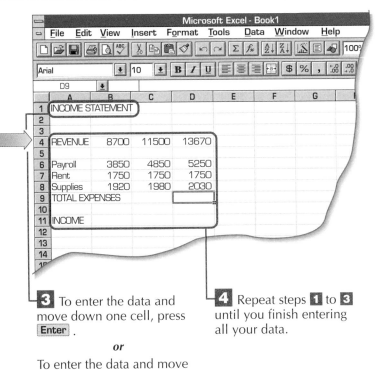

3 To enter the data and move down one cell, press Enter .

or

To enter the data and move one cell in any direction, press →, ←, ↓ or ↑ .

4 Repeat steps **1** to **3** until you finish entering all your data.

LONG LABELS

8		
9	TOTAL EXPENSES	
10		

◆ If a label you type is too long to fit in one cell, the text will spill over into neighboring cells if they are empty.

8		
9	TOTAL EX	227
10		

◆ If the neighboring cell contains data, Excel will display as much of the label as the column width will allow.

LONG NUMBERS

8		
9	1.22E+10	
10	######	

◆ If a number you type is too long to fit in one cell, Excel will display it in scientific form or number signs (###) will appear in the cell.

Note: To display an entire label or number, you must increase the column width. For more information, refer to page 82.

SELECT CELLS

Before you can use many Excel features, you must first select the cells you want to work with. Selected cells appear highlighted on your screen.

SELECT A ROW

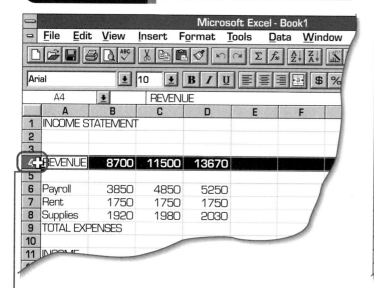

1 Move the mouse ⊹ over the row number you want to select (example: **4**) and then press the left button.

◆ Make sure the mouse looks like ⊹ (not ‡) before pressing the button.

TO CANCEL A SELECTION

Move the mouse ⊹ over any cell in your worksheet and then press the left button.

SELECT A COLUMN

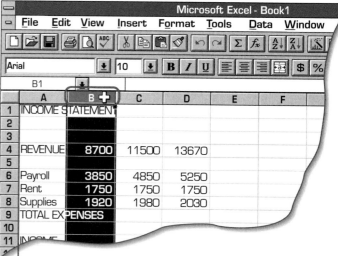

1 Move the mouse ⊹ over the column letter you want to select (example: **B**) and then press the left button.

◆ Make sure the mouse looks like ⊹ (not ↔) before pressing the button.

SELECT THE ENTIRE WORKSHEET

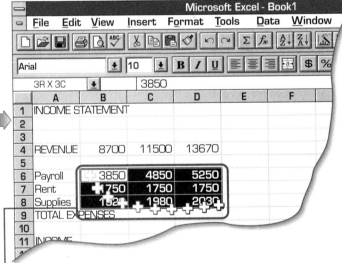

1 Move the mouse ⊹ over the area where the row and column headings intersect and then press the left button.

SELECT A GROUP OF CELLS

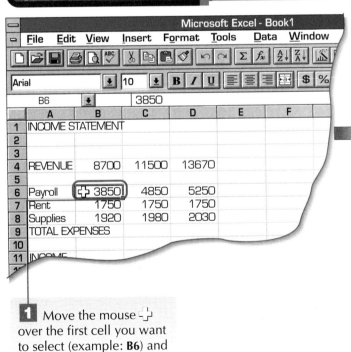

1 Move the mouse ⊹ over the first cell you want to select (example: **B6**) and then press and hold down the left button.

2 Still holding down the button, drag the mouse ⊹ until you highlight all the cells you want to select.

3 Release the button.

SELECT TWO GROUPS OF CELLS

To select another group of cells, press and hold down Ctrl while repeating steps **1** to **3**.

13

USING AUTOFILL

You can save time by using the AutoFill feature to complete a series of labels or numbers in your worksheet.

USING AUTOFILL TO COMPLETE A SERIES

Complete a Series of Labels

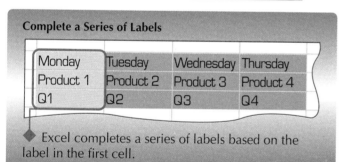

Monday	Tuesday	Wednesday	Thursday
Product 1	Product 2	Product 3	Product 4
Q1	Q2	Q3	Q4

◆ Excel completes a series of labels based on the label in the first cell.

Complete a Series of Numbers

1993	1994	1995	1996
1	2	3	4
5	10	15	20

◆ Excel completes a series of numbers based on the numbers in the first two cells. These numbers tell Excel how much to add to each number to complete the series.

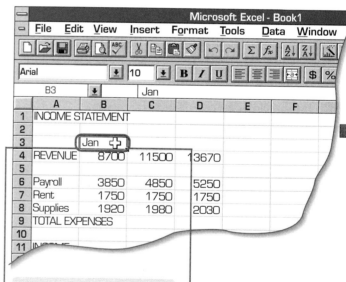

1 To create a series of labels, type and enter the first label in the series (example: **Jan**).

◆ To create a series of numbers, type and enter the first two numbers in the series.

2 Select the cell(s) containing the label or numbers you entered.

Note: To select cells, refer to page 12.

Getting Started	Save and Open Your Workbooks	Edit Your Worksheets	Using Formulas and Functions	Working with Rows and Columns	Format Your Worksheets	Smart Formatting	Print Your Worksheets

- Introduction
- Using the Mouse
- Start Excel
- Excel Basics
- Enter Data
- Select Cells

- **Using AutoFill**
- Using the Menus
- The Toolbars
- Move Through a Worksheet
- Getting Help

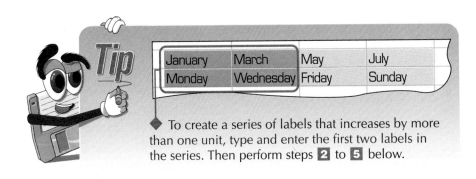

◆ To create a series of labels that increases by more than one unit, type and enter the first two labels in the series. Then perform steps **2** to **5** below.

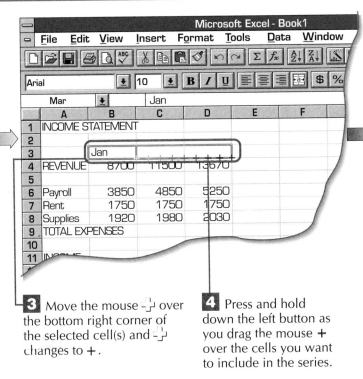

3 Move the mouse over the bottom right corner of the selected cell(s) and changes to +.

4 Press and hold down the left button as you drag the mouse + over the cells you want to include in the series.

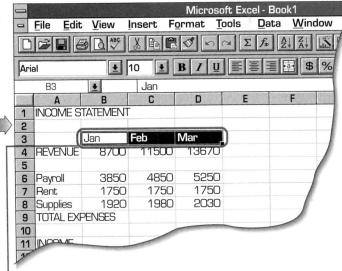

5 Release the button and the cells display the series.

Note: You can also use the AutoFill feature to fill data in columns.

USING THE MENUS

You can open a menu to display a list of related commands. You can then select the command you want to use.

USING THE MENUS

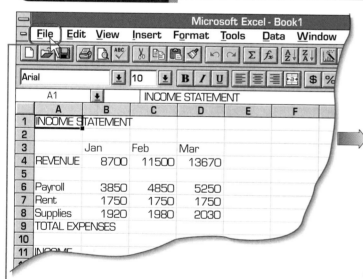

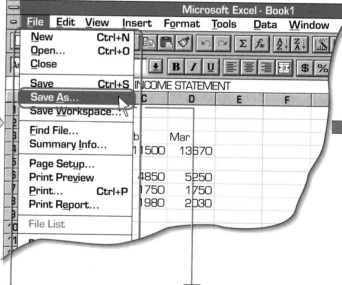

1 To open a menu, move the mouse ⬧ over the menu name (example: **File**) and then press the left button.

◆ A menu appears, displaying a list of related commands.

Note: To close a menu, move the mouse ⬧ anywhere over your worksheet and then press the left button.

2 To select a command, move the mouse ⬧ over the command name (example: **Save As**) and then press the left button.

Getting Started	Save and Open Your Workbooks	Edit Your Worksheets	Using Formulas and Functions	Working with Rows and Columns	Format Your Worksheets	Smart Formatting	Print Your Worksheets

- Introduction
- Using the Mouse
- Start Excel
- Excel Basics
- Enter Data
- Select Cells

- Using AutoFill
- **Using the Menus**
- The Toolbars
- Move Through a Worksheet
- Getting Help

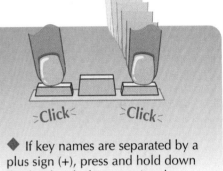

Tips

Edit	
Can't Undo	Ctrl+Z
Can't Repeat	F4
Cut	Ctrl+X
Copy	Ctrl+C
Paste	Ctrl+V
Paste Special...	
Fill	▶

◆ If a command is dimmed (example: **Paste**), it is currently unavailable.

◆ If key names are separated by a plus sign (+), press and hold down the first key before pressing the second key (example: Ctrl + C).

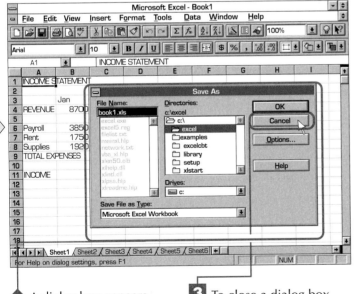

◆ A dialog box appears if Excel requires more information to carry out the command.

3 To close a dialog box, move the mouse ⋏ over **Cancel** and then press the left button.

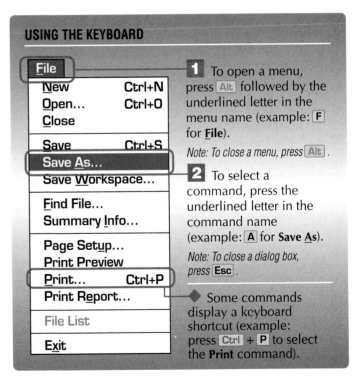

USING THE KEYBOARD

1 To open a menu, press Alt followed by the underlined letter in the menu name (example: F for **File**).

Note: To close a menu, press Alt .

2 To select a command, press the underlined letter in the command name (example: A for **Save As**).

Note: To close a dialog box, press Esc .

◆ Some commands display a keyboard shortcut (example: press Ctrl + P to select the **Print** command).

THE TOOLBARS

> A toolbar contains a series of buttons that let you quickly select commonly used commands. You can receive help information on any of these buttons.

THE TOOLBARS

The buttons on a toolbar save you time by providing quick methods of selecting menu commands.

For example, you can use  to quickly select the Save command.

File	
New	Ctrl+N
Open...	Ctrl+O
Close	
Save	Ctrl+S
Save **A**s...	
Save **W**orkspace...	
Find File...	

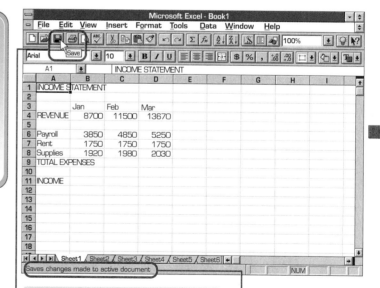

1 To display a description of a button displayed on your screen, move the mouse ⌖ over the button of interest (example: 💾).

◆ After a few seconds, the name of the button appears in a yellow box.

◆ A short description of the button also appears at the bottom of your screen.

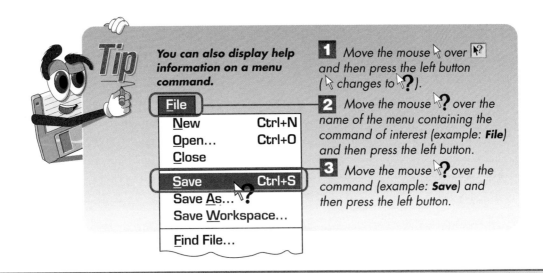

Tip

You can also display help information on a menu command.

File	
New	Ctrl+N
Open...	Ctrl+O
Close	
Save	Ctrl+S
Save As...	
Save Workspace...	
Find File...	

1 Move the mouse over and then press the left button (changes to **?**).

2 Move the mouse **?** over the name of the menu containing the command of interest (example: **File**) and then press the left button.

3 Move the mouse **?** over the command (example: **Save**) and then press the left button.

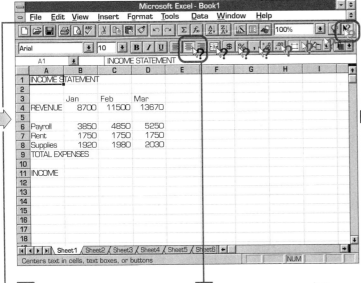

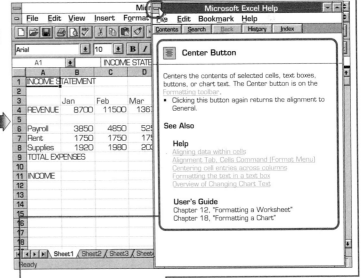

2 To display detailed help information on a button, move the mouse over and then press the left button (changes to **?**).

3 Move the mouse **?** over the button of interest (example:) and then press the left button.

◆ Information on the button you selected appears.

4 To close the **Microsoft Excel Help** window, move the mouse over and then quickly press the left button twice.

MOVE THROUGH A WORKSHEET

If your worksheet contains a lot of data, your computer screen cannot display all of the data at the same time. You must scroll up or down to view other parts of your worksheet.

MOVE TO CELL A1

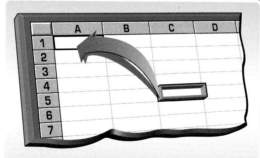

◆ Press `Ctrl` + `Home` to move to cell **A1** from any cell in your worksheet.

MOVE ONE SCREEN UP OR DOWN

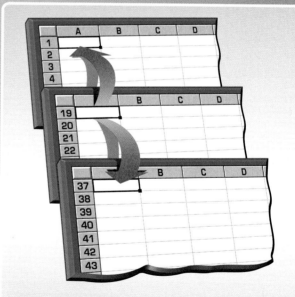

◆ Press `PageDown` to move down one screen.

◆ Press `PageUp` to move up one screen.

◆ Press `Alt` + `PageDown` to move right one screen.

◆ Press `Alt` + `PageUp` to move left one screen.

SCROLL UP OR DOWN

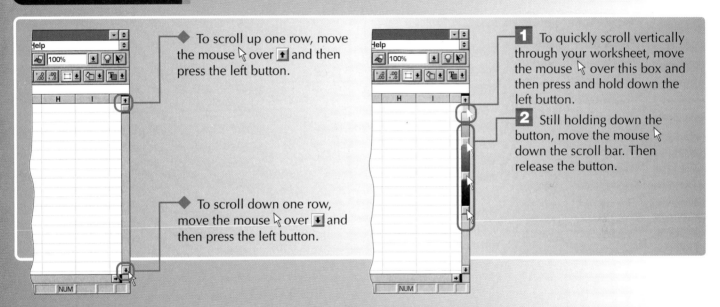

To scroll up one row, move the mouse over ↑ and then press the left button.

To scroll down one row, move the mouse over ↓ and then press the left button.

1 To quickly scroll vertically through your worksheet, move the mouse over this box and then press and hold down the left button.

2 Still holding down the button, move the mouse down the scroll bar. Then release the button.

SCROLL LEFT OR RIGHT

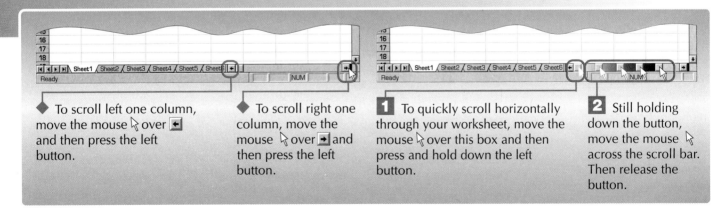

To scroll left one column, move the mouse over ← and then press the left button.

To scroll right one column, move the mouse over → and then press the left button.

1 To quickly scroll horizontally through your worksheet, move the mouse over this box and then press and hold down the left button.

2 Still holding down the button, move the mouse across the scroll bar. Then release the button.

GETTING HELP

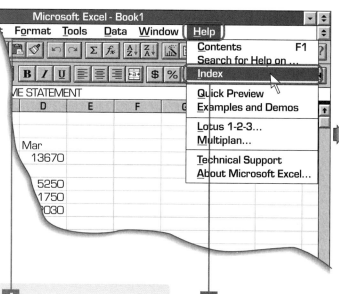

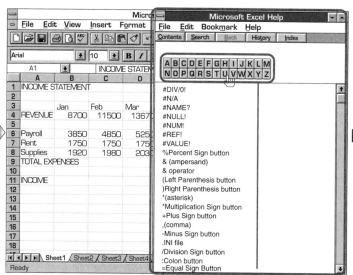

◆ The **Microsoft Excel Help** window appears.

1 To display the Microsoft Excel Help Index, move the mouse over **Help** and then press the left button.

2 Move the mouse over **Index** and then press the left button.

3 Move the mouse over the first letter of the topic you want information on (example: **U** for **Underlining**) and then press the left button.

Getting Started	Save and Open Your Workbooks	Edit Your Worksheets	Using Formulas and Functions	Working with Rows and Columns	Format Your Worksheets	Smart Formatting	Print Your Worksheets

- Introduction
- Using the Mouse
- Start Excel
- Excel Basics
- Enter Data
- Select Cells

- Using AutoFill
- Using the Menus
- The Toolbars
- Move Through a Worksheet
- **Getting Help**

THE TIPWIZARD

If Excel knows a better way to accomplish a task you are performing, the TipWizard button will turn from white to yellow.

1 To display the tip, move the mouse over and then press the left button. The tip appears.

Note: To hide the tip, repeat step **1**.

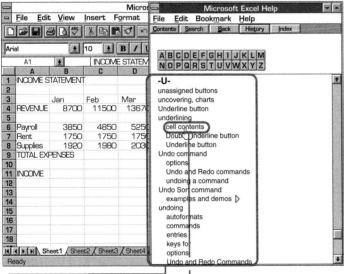

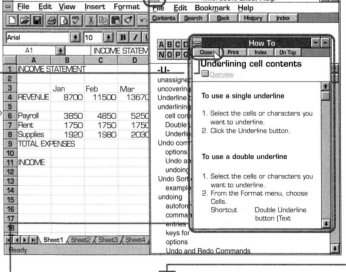

◆ Topics beginning with the letter you selected appear.

◆ To view more topics beginning with the letter, press `PageDown` on your keyboard.

4 Move the mouse over the topic of interest and then press the left button.

◆ Information on the topic you selected appears.

5 To close the **How To** window, move the mouse over **Close** and then press the left button.

6 To close the **Microsoft Excel Help** window, move the mouse over and then quickly press the left button twice.

23

SAVE AND OPEN YOUR WORKBOOKS

◆ In this chapter, you will learn how to save your work and exit Excel. You will also learn to find and open your workbooks.

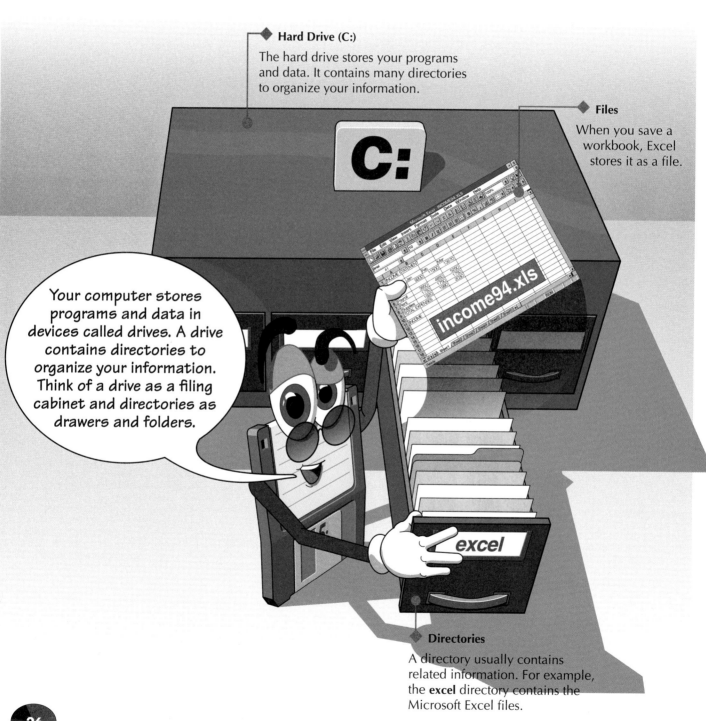

Hard Drive (C:)

The hard drive stores your programs and data. It contains many directories to organize your information.

Files

When you save a workbook, Excel stores it as a file.

Your computer stores programs and data in devices called drives. A drive contains directories to organize your information. Think of a drive as a filing cabinet and directories as drawers and folders.

income94.xls

excel

Directories

A directory usually contains related information. For example, the **excel** directory contains the Microsoft Excel files.

Most computers have one hard drive and one or two floppy drives to store information.

Hard drive (C:)

◆ The hard drive magnetically stores information inside your computer. It is called drive **C**.

*Note: Your computer may be set up to have additional hard drives (example: drive **D**).*

Floppy drives (A: and B:)

◆ A floppy drive stores information on removable diskettes (or floppy disks). A diskette operates slower and stores less data than a hard drive.

◆ **Diskettes are used to:**

- Load new programs.
- Store backup copies of data.
- Transfer data to other computers.

If your computer has only one floppy drive, it is called drive **A**.

If your computer has two floppy drives, the second drive is called drive **B**.

SAVE A WORKBOOK

You should save your workbook to store it for future use. This lets you later retrieve the workbook for reviewing or editing purposes.

SAVE A WORKBOOK

When you save a workbook for the first time, you must give it a name. A file name consists of two parts: a name and an extension. You must separate these parts with a period.

INCOME94.XLS

♦ **Name**

The name should describe the contents of a workbook. It can have up to eight characters.

♦ **Period**

A period must separate the name and the extension.

♦ **Extension**

The extension describes the type of information a workbook contains. It can have up to three characters.

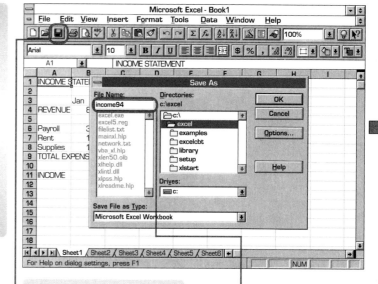

1 Move the mouse over ![save] and then press the left button.

♦ The **Save As** dialog box appears.

Note: If you previously saved your workbook, the Save As dialog box will not appear since you have already named the file.

2 Type a name for your workbook (example: **income94**) and then press **Enter**.

Note: To make it easier to find your workbook later on, do not type an extension. Excel will automatically add the xls extension to the file name.

| Getting Started | Save and Open Your Workbooks | Edit Your Worksheets | Using Formulas and Functions | Working with Rows and Columns | Format Your Worksheets | Smart Formatting | Print Your Worksheets |

- Introduction
- **Save a Workbook**
- Save a Workbook to a Diskette
- Exit Excel
- Open a Workbook
- Find a Workbook

Rules for Naming a File

A file name *can* contain the following characters:

- The letters A to Z, upper or lower case
- The numbers 0 to 9
- The symbols
  _ ^ $ ~ ! # % & { } @ ( )

A file name *cannot* contain the following characters:

- A comma (,)
- A blank space
- The symbols
  * ? ; [ ] + = \ / : < >

Each file in a directory must have a unique name.

income94.xls
report.xls
taxes.xls

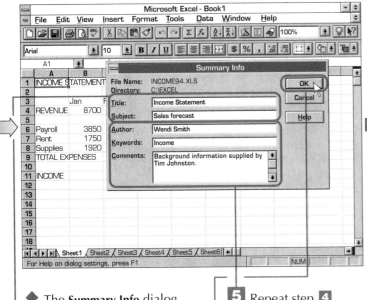

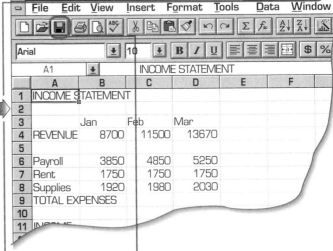

◆ The **Summary Info** dialog box appears.

3 Type a title for your workbook.

4 Press **Tab** to move to the next category. Type the corresponding information.

5 Repeat step **4** until you have typed all the information.

6 Move the mouse over **OK** and then press the left button.

◆ Excel saves your workbook and displays the name at the top of your screen.

◆ You should save your workbook every 10 to 15 minutes to store any changes made since the last time you saved the workbook. To save changes, move the mouse over and then press the left button.

SAVE A WORKBOOK TO A DISKETTE

As a precaution, you should save your workbook to a diskette. You can then use this copy to replace any lost data if your hard drive fails or you accidentally erase the file.

SAVE A WORKBOOK TO A DISKETTE

1 Insert a diskette into a floppy drive (example: **drive a**).

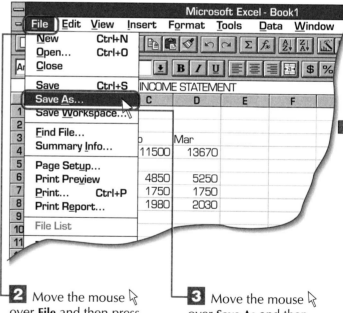

2 Move the mouse ⌖ over **File** and then press the left button.

3 Move the mouse ⌖ over **Save As** and then press the left button.

SAVE A WORKBOOK WITH A NEW NAME

After you save your workbook, you may want to make additional changes. In case you regret any of these changes, you can keep a copy of the old version by saving the workbook with a new name.

1 Perform steps **2** to **4** below.

2 Move the mouse ⇖ over **OK** and then press the left button.

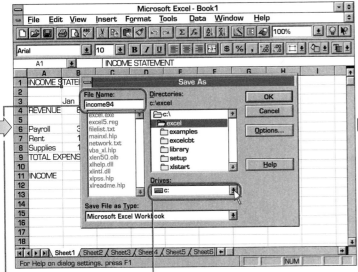

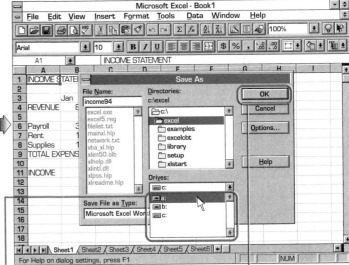

◆ The **Save As** dialog box appears.

4 The **File Name**: box displays the current file name. To save your workbook with a different name, type a new name.

◆ The **Drives**: box displays the current drive (example: **c:**).

5 To save the file to a different drive, move the mouse ⇖ over ⬇ in the **Drives**: box and then press the left button.

◆ A list of the available drives for your computer appears.

6 Move the mouse ⇖ over the drive you want to use (example: **a:**) and then press the left button.

7 To save your workbook, move the mouse ⇖ over **OK** and then press the left button.

EXIT EXCEL

When you finish using Excel, you can exit the program to return to the Windows Program Manager.

EXIT EXCEL

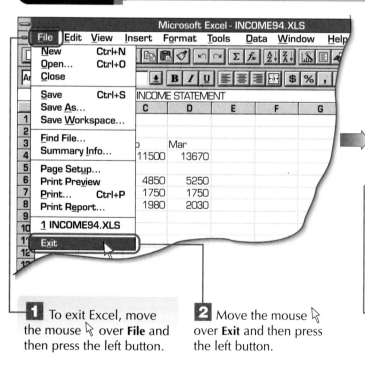

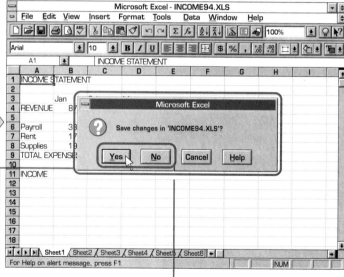

1 To exit Excel, move the mouse ⌖ over **File** and then press the left button.

2 Move the mouse ⌖ over **Exit** and then press the left button.

◆ This dialog box appears if you have not saved changes made to your workbook.

3 To save your workbook before exiting, move the mouse ⌖ over **Yes** and then press the left button.

◆ To exit without saving your workbook, move the mouse ⌖ over **No** and then press the left button.

| Getting Started | Save and Open Your Workbooks | Edit Your Worksheets | Using Formulas and Functions | Working with Rows and Columns | Format Your Worksheets | Smart Formatting | Print Your Worksheets |

- Introduction
- Save a Workbook
- Save a Workbook to a Diskette
- **Exit Excel**
- Open a Workbook
- Find a Workbook

IMPORTANT!

You must always exit Excel and Windows before turning off your computer. Failure to do so may result in damage or loss of valuable information.

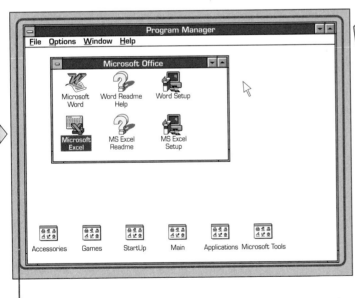

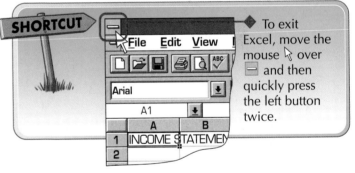

SHORTCUT

To exit Excel, move the mouse over ⊟ and then quickly press the left button twice.

◆ The **Program Manager** window appears.

Note: To restart Excel, refer to page 6.

OPEN A WORKBOOK

You can open a saved workbook and display it on your screen. This lets you review and edit the workbook.

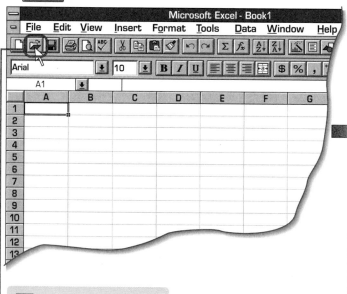

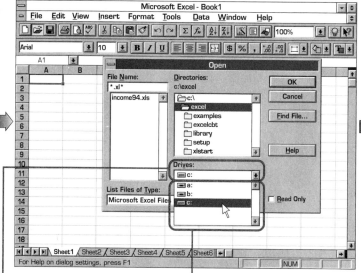

1 Move the mouse ⤢ over and then press the left button.

◆ The **Open** dialog box appears.

◆ The **Drives**: box displays the current drive (example: **c:**).

2 To open a file on a different drive, move the mouse ⤢ over ▣ in the **Drives**: box and then press the left button.

◆ A list of the available drives for your computer appears.

3 Move the mouse ⤢ over the drive containing the file you want to open and then press the left button.

| Getting Started | Save and Open Your Workbooks | Edit Your Worksheets | Using Formulas and Functions | Working with Rows and Columns | Format Your Worksheets | Smart Formatting | Print Your Worksheets |

- Introduction
- Save a Workbook
- Save a Workbook to a Diskette
- Exit Excel
- **Open a Workbook**
- Find a Workbook

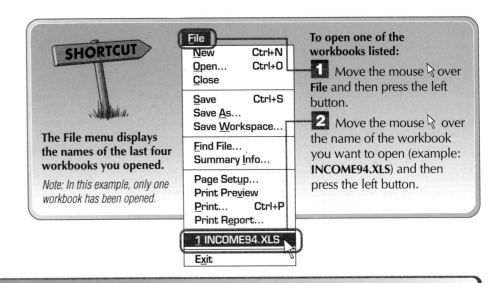

SHORTCUT

The File menu displays the names of the last four workbooks you opened.

Note: In this example, only one workbook has been opened.

To open one of the workbooks listed:

1 Move the mouse Ⓚ over **File** and then press the left button.

2 Move the mouse Ⓚ over the name of the workbook you want to open (example: **INCOME94.XLS**) and then press the left button.

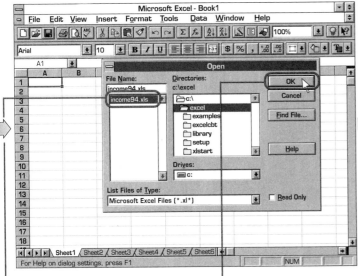

4 Move the mouse Ⓚ over the name of the file you want to open (example: **income94.xls**) and then press the left button.

Note: If you cannot remember the location of the file you want to open, refer to page 36 to find the file.

5 Move the mouse Ⓚ over **OK** and then press the left button.

◆ Excel opens the workbook and displays it on your screen. You can now make changes to the workbook.

◆ The name of the workbook appears at the top of your screen.

FIND A WORKBOOK

If you cannot remember the location of the workbook you want to open, you can use the Find File feature to search for the workbook.

FIND A WORKBOOK

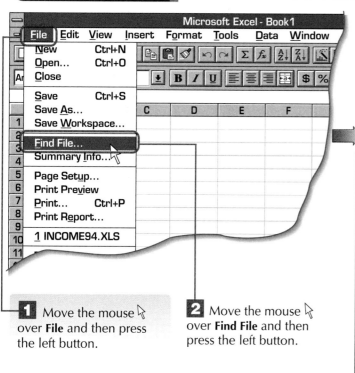

1 Move the mouse ☐ over **File** and then press the left button.

2 Move the mouse ☐ over **Find File** and then press the left button.

◆ The **Search** dialog box appears.

*Note: If the **Find File** dialog box appears, see IMPORTANT at the top of page 37.*

3 To remove the characters in the **File Name:** box, press `Delete` on your keyboard.

4 To search for a file with a particular extension, type ***.** followed by the extension. For example, type ***.xls** to find all files with the **xls** extension.

◆ To search for a file that begins with a particular sequence of letters, type the letters followed by the ***.*** characters. For example, type **n*.*** to find all files starting with **n**.

36

| Getting Started | Save and Open Your Workbooks | Edit Your Worksheets | Using Formulas and Functions | Working with Rows and Columns | Format Your Worksheets | Smart Formatting | Print Your Worksheets |

- Introduction
- Save a Workbook
- Save a Workbook to a Diskette
- Exit Excel
- Open a Workbook
- **Find a Workbook**

IMPORTANT!

The Find File dialog box appears if you have previously used the Find File command. To start a new search:

1 Move the mouse over **Search** and then press the left button. The **Search** dialog box appears.

Search...

2 To clear all the options you set for your last search, move the mouse over **Clear** and then press the left button.

Clear

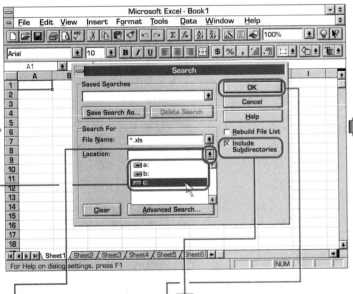

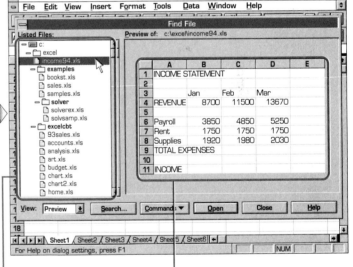

5 To select the drive you want to search, move the mouse over ⬇ beside the **Location:** box and then press the left button.

6 Move the mouse over the drive (example: **c:**) and then press the left button.

7 To search all subdirectories on the drive you selected, move the mouse over **Include Subdirectories** and then press the left button (□ changes to ⊠).

8 To start the search, move the mouse over **OK** and then press the left button.

◆ After a few moments, the **Find File** dialog box appears.

◆ This area displays the names of the files Excel found.

◆ This area displays the contents of the highlighted file.

9 To display the contents of another file, press ⬇ or ⬆ on your keyboard.

10 To open a file, move the mouse over its name and then quickly press the left button twice.

verview

EDIT YOUR WORKSHEETS

Edit Data

Clear Data

Undo Last Change

Insert Cells

Delete Cells

Move Data

Copy Data

Check Spelling

◆ In this chapter, you will learn how to make changes to data in your worksheet.

EDIT DATA

After you enter data into your worksheet, you can correct a typing error or revise the data.

EDIT DATA IN A CELL

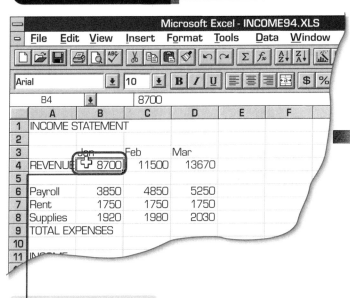

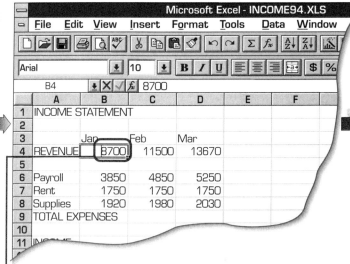

1 Move the mouse 🔁 over the cell containing the data you want to change (example: **B4**) and then quickly press the left button twice.

◆ A flashing insertion point appears in the cell.

2 Move the mouse I over the position where you want to add or delete characters and then press the left button.

Note: You can also press → or ← on your keyboard to move the insertion point.

Getting Started

Save and Open Your Workbooks

Edit Your Worksheets

Using Formulas and Functions

Working with Rows and Columns

Format Your Worksheets

Smart Formatting

Print Your Worksheets

- **Edit Data**
- Clear Data
- Undo Last Change
- Insert Cells
- Delete Cells
- Move Data
- Copy Data
- Check Spelling

REPLACE ENTIRE CELL CONTENTS

You can completely replace the contents of a cell with new data.

8700

1 Move the mouse ✛ over the cell containing the data you want to replace with new data and then press the left button.

9245

2 Type the new data and then press Enter.

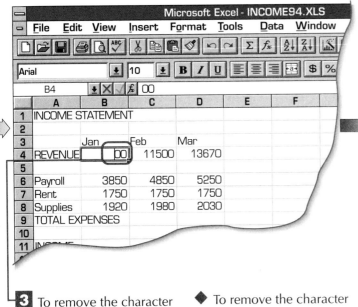

3 To remove the character to the right of the insertion point, press Delete.

◆ To remove the character to the left of the insertion point, press ←Backspace.

4 To insert data where the insertion point flashes on your screen, type the data.

5 When you finish making the changes, press Enter.

CLEAR DATA UNDO LAST CHANGE

You can completely erase the contents of cells in your worksheet.

CLEAR DATA

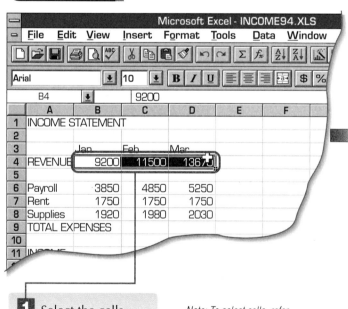

1 Select the cells containing the data you want to remove.

Note: To select cells, refer to page 12.

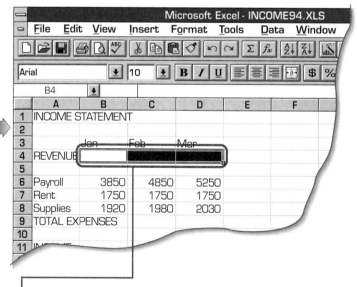

2 Press **Delete** and the contents of the cells you selected disappear.

42

Getting Started	Save and Open Your Workbooks	Edit Your Worksheets	Using Formulas and Functions	Working with Rows and Columns	Format Your Worksheets	Smart Formatting	Print Your Worksheets

- Edit Data
- **Clear Data**
- **Undo Last Change**
- Insert Cells
- Delete Cells
- Move Data
- Copy Data
- Check Spelling

Excel remembers the last change you made to your worksheet. If you regret this change, you can cancel it by using the Undo feature.

UNDO YOUR LAST CHANGE

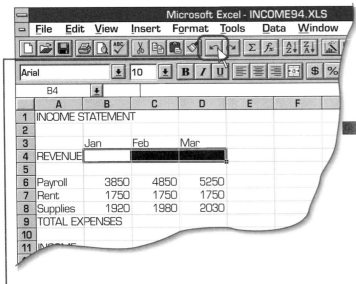

1 To cancel the last change made to your worksheet, move the mouse ⌖ over ▣ and then press the left button.

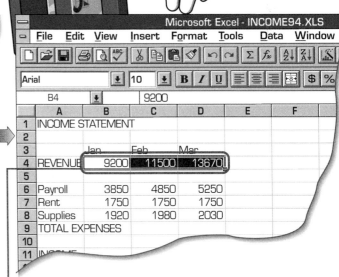

◆ Excel cancels your last change.

INSERT CELLS

If you want to add new data to your worksheet you can insert cells. The surrounding cells move to make room for the new cells.

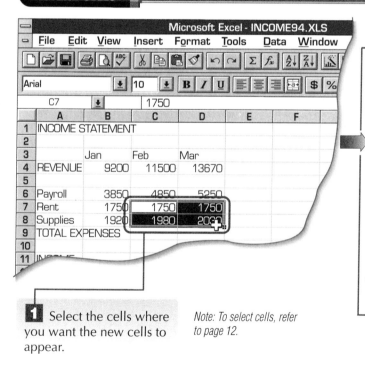

1 Select the cells where you want the new cells to appear.

Note: To select cells, refer to page 12.

2 Move the mouse over **Insert** and then press the left button.

3 Move the mouse over **Cells** and then press the left button.

◆ The **Insert** dialog box appears.

44

Getting Started	Save and Open Your Workbooks	**Edit Your Worksheets**	Using Formulas and Functions	Working with Rows and Columns	Format Your Worksheets	Smart Formatting	Print Your Worksheets

- Edit Data
- Clear Data
- Undo Last Change
- **Insert Cells**

- Delete Cells
- Move Data
- Copy Data
- Check Spelling

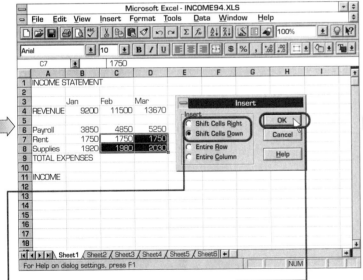

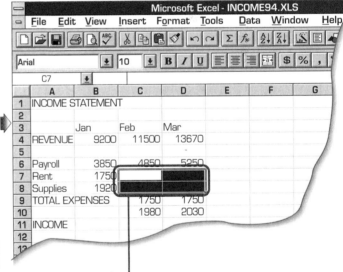

4 To move the selected cells downward, move the mouse ⍩ over **Shift Cells Down** and then press the left button.

◆ To move the selected cells to the right, move the mouse ⍩ over **Shift Cells Right** and then press the left button.

5 Move the mouse ⍩ over **OK** and then press the left button.

◆ The new cells appear. The cells you selected move to make room for the new cells.

DELETE CELLS

You can remove cells you no longer need in your worksheet. The surrounding cells move to fill the empty space.

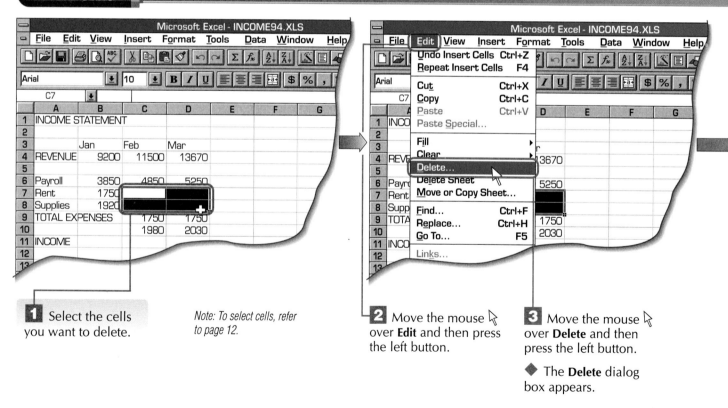

1 Select the cells you want to delete.

Note: To select cells, refer to page 12.

2 Move the mouse over **Edit** and then press the left button.

3 Move the mouse over **Delete** and then press the left button.

◆ The **Delete** dialog box appears.

INTRODUCTION TO EXCEL

| Getting Started | Save and Open Your Workbooks | **Edit Your Worksheets** | Using Formulas and Functions | Working with Rows and Columns | Format Your Worksheets | Smart Formatting | Print Your Worksheets |

- Edit Data
- Clear Data
- Undo Last Change
- Insert Cells

- **Delete Cells**
- Move Data
- Copy Data
- Check Spelling

Tip

The Delete and Clear features both remove data from your worksheet. However, there is one distinct difference.

◆ The **Delete** feature removes cells and their contents.

◆ The **Clear** feature removes only the contents of cells.

Note: For information on the Clear feature, refer to page 42.

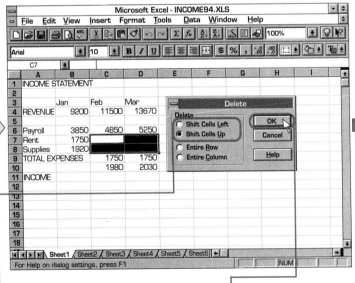

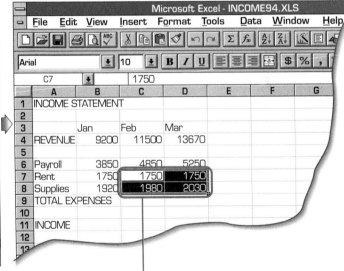

4 To move the surrounding cells upward, move the mouse �️ over **Shift Cells Up** and then press the left button.

◆ To move the surrounding cells to the left, move the mouse �️ over **Shift Cells Left** and then press the left button.

5 Move the mouse �️ over **OK** and then press the left button.

◆ The cells you selected disappear. The surrounding cells move to fill the empty space.

MOVE DATA

You can move data from one location in your worksheet to another. Excel cuts the data and pastes it in a new location. The original data disappears.

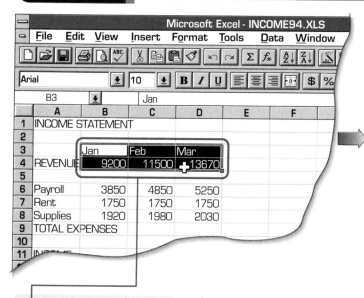

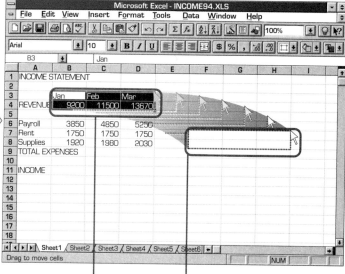

1 Select the cells containing the data you want to move to a new location.

Note: To select cells, refer to page 12.

2 Move the mouse ⊹ over any border of the selected cells and ⊹ changes to ↖.

3 Press and hold down the left button and then drag the mouse ↖ where you want to place the data.

◆ A rectangular box indicates where the data will appear.

48

| Getting Started | Save and Open Your Workbooks | Edit Your Worksheets | Using Formulas and Functions | Working with Rows and Columns | Format Your Worksheets | Smart Formatting | Print Your Worksheets |

- Edit Data
- Clear Data
- Undo Last Change
- Insert Cells

- Delete Cells
- **Move Data**
- Copy Data
- Check Spelling

Tip

You can also move data to another worksheet.

Note: For more information, refer to page 152.

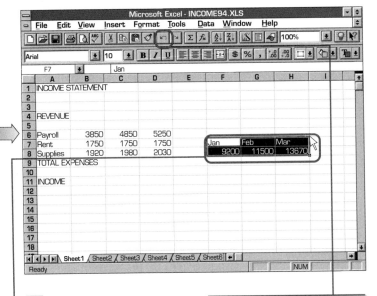

4 Release the left button and the data moves to the new location.

CANCEL THE MOVE

◆ To immediately cancel the move, position the mouse over and then press the left button.

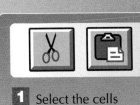

You can also use these buttons to move data.

1 Select the cells containing the data you want to move to a new location.

2 Move the mouse over and then press the left button.

3 Select the cell where you want to place the data. This cell will become the top left cell of the new location.

4 Move the mouse over and then press the left button. The data appears in the new location.

COPY DATA

You can copy data from one location in your worksheet to another. Excel copies the data and pastes it in a new location. The original data remains in its place.

COPY DATA

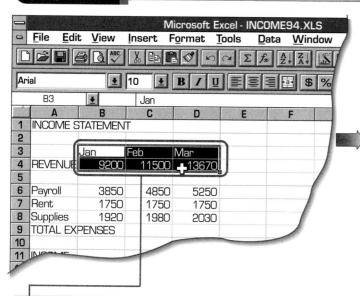

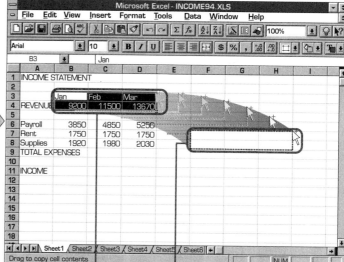

1 Select the cells containing the data you want to copy to a new location.

Note: To select cells, refer to page 12.

2 Move the mouse ⌖ over any border of the selected cells (⌖ changes to ⇦).

3 Press and hold down `Ctrl` and the left button (⇦ changes to ⇦).

4 Still holding down `Ctrl` and the left button, drag the mouse ⇦ where you want to place the data.

◆ A rectangular box indicates where the data will appear.

50

Getting Started	Save and Open Your Workbooks	Edit Your Worksheets	Using Formulas and Functions	Working with Rows and Columns	Format Your Worksheets	Smart Formatting	Print Your Worksheets

- Edit Data
- Clear Data
- Undo Last Change
- Insert Cells

- Delete Cells
- Move Data
- **Copy Data**
- Check Spelling

Tip

You can also copy data to another worksheet.

Note: For more information, refer to page 152.

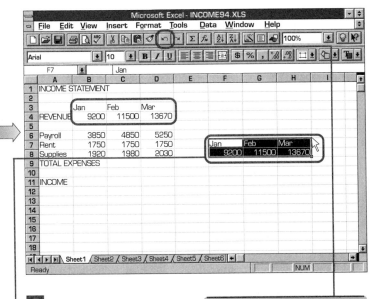

You can also use these buttons to copy data.

1 Select the cells containing the data you want to copy to a new location.

2 Move the mouse over and then press the left button.

3 Select the cell where you want to place the data. This cell will become the top left cell of the new location.

4 Move the mouse over and then press the left button. A copy of the data appears in the new location.

Note: You can repeat steps **3** and **4** to place the data in multiple locations in your worksheet.

5 Release the left button and then release Ctrl.

◆ A copy of the data appears in the new location.

CANCEL THE COPY

◆ To immediately cancel the copy, position the mouse over and then press the left button.

CHECK SPELLING

You can use Excel's spelling feature to find and correct spelling errors in your worksheet.

Excel compares every word in your worksheet to words in its own dictionary. If a word does not exist in the dictionary, Excel considers it misspelled.

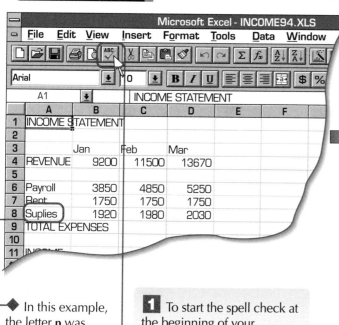

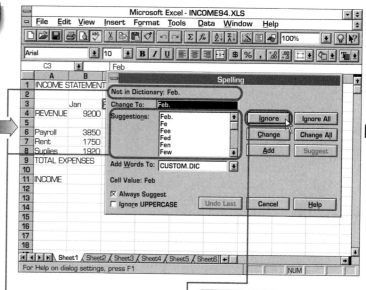

◆ In this example, the letter **p** was removed from **Supplies**.

1 To start the spell check at the beginning of your worksheet, press `Ctrl` + `Home` to move to cell **A1**.

*Note: To spell check a section of your worksheet, select the cells before performing step **2**. To select cells, refer to page 12.*

2 Move the mouse ⟲ over ABC and then press the left button.

◆ If Excel finds a spelling error, the **Spelling** dialog box appears.

◆ Excel displays the word it does not recognize and suggestions to correct the error.

Ignore misspelled word

3 If you do not want to change the spelling of the word, move the mouse ⟲ over **Ignore** and then press the left button.

INTRODUCTION TO EXCEL

| Getting Started | Save and Open Your Workbooks | **Edit Your Worksheets** | Using Formulas and Functions | Working with Rows and Columns | Format Your Worksheets | Smart Formatting | Print Your Worksheets |

- Edit Data
- Clear Data
- Undo Last Change
- Insert Cells
- Delete Cells
- Move Data
- Copy Data
- **Check Spelling**

SPELL CHECK OPTIONS

When Excel finds a spelling error in your worksheet, you can choose one of the following options.

Ignore Keeps the current spelling of the word in this instance only.

Change Replaces the misspelled word in your worksheet with the text in the **Change To**: box.

Add Adds the word to Excel's dictionary. The spell check then considers the word correctly spelled in all future spell checks.

Ignore All Keeps the current spelling of the word and skips every occurrence in the worksheet.

Change All Replaces the misspelled word with the text in the **Change To**: box every time it appears in your worksheet.

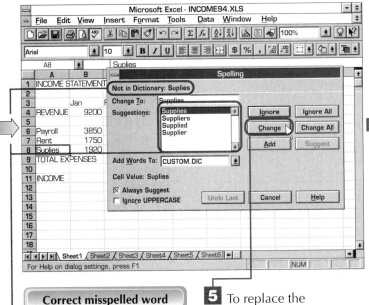

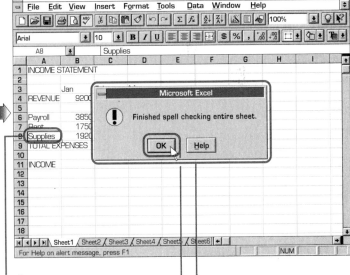

Correct misspelled word

◆ Excel displays the next word it does not recognize.

4 To correct the spelling, move the mouse �️ over the word you want to use and then press the left button.

5 To replace the misspelled word in your worksheet with the correct spelling, move the mouse �️ over **Change** and then press the left button.

◆ Excel corrects the word and continues checking for spelling errors.

6 Ignore or correct spelling errors until Excel finishes checking your worksheet.

◆ This dialog box appears when the spell check is complete.

7 To close the dialog box, move the mouse �️ over **OK** and then press the left button.

USING FORMULAS AND FUNCTIONS

Formulas

Enter a Formula

Functions

Enter a Function

Add Numbers

Errors in Formulas

Copy Formulas

Name Cells

◆ In this chapter, you will learn how to enter formulas into your worksheet. This lets you perform calculations on your worksheet data.

FORMULAS

You can use formulas to perform calculations on your worksheet data.

INTRODUCTION TO FORMULAS

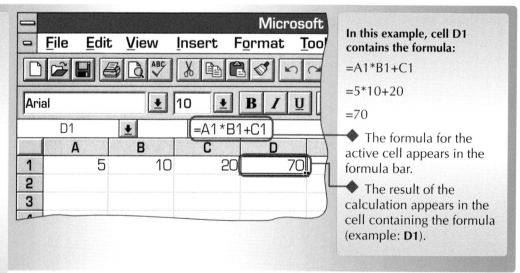

◆ You must begin a formula with an equal sign (=).

◆ You should use cell references (example: **A1**) instead of actual numbers whenever possible. This way, if your data changes, Excel will automatically redo the calculations.

◆ Excel will perform calculations in the following order:

1 Exponentiation

2 Multiplication and Division

3 Addition and Subtraction

In this example, cell D1 contains the formula:

=A1*B1+C1

=5*10+20

=70

◆ The formula for the active cell appears in the formula bar.

◆ The result of the calculation appears in the cell containing the formula (example: **D1**).

INTRODUCTION TO EXCEL

| Getting Started | Save and Open Your Workbooks | Edit Your Worksheets | Using Formulas and Functions | Working with Rows and Columns | Format Your Worksheets | Smart Formatting | Print Your Worksheets |

• **Formulas**
• Enter a Formula
• Functions
• Enter a Function

• Add Numbers
• Errors in Formulas
• Copy Formulas
• Name Cells

You can use these operators in your formulas:

+	Addition
-	Subtraction
*	Multiplication
/	Division
^	Exponentiation

You can change the order that Excel calculates your formulas by using parentheses ( ).

◆ Excel will calculate the numbers in parentheses first.

In this example, cell D1 contains the formula:

=A1*(B1+C1)

=5*(10+20)

=150

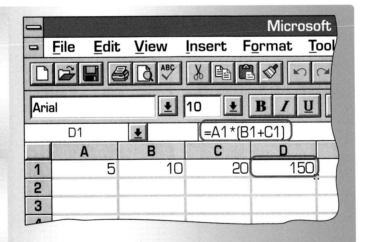

ENTER A FORMULA

You can enter a formula into any cell in your worksheet.

ENTER A FORMULA

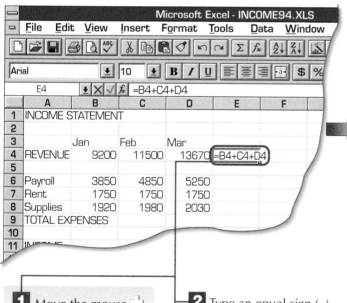

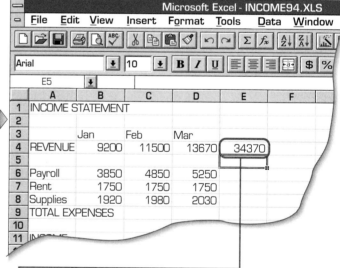

1 Move the mouse ⊕ over the cell where you want to enter a formula (example: **E4**) and then press the left button.

2 Type an equal sign (=) to begin the formula.

3 Type the calculation you want to perform (example: **B4+C4+D4**).

Note: This formula will calculate the total Revenue.

4 Press **Enter** and the result of the calculation appears in the cell (example: **34370**).

INTRODUCTION TO EXCEL

| Getting Started | Save and Open Your Workbooks | Edit Your Worksheets | Using Formulas and Functions | Working with Rows and Columns | Format Your Worksheets | Smart Formatting | Print Your Worksheets |

• Formulas
• **Enter a Formula**
• Functions
• Enter a Function

• Add Numbers
• Errors in Formulas
• Copy Formulas
• Name Cells

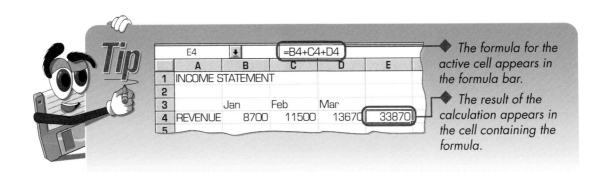

Tip

◆ The formula for the active cell appears in the formula bar.

◆ The result of the calculation appears in the cell containing the formula.

AUTOMATIC RECALCULATION

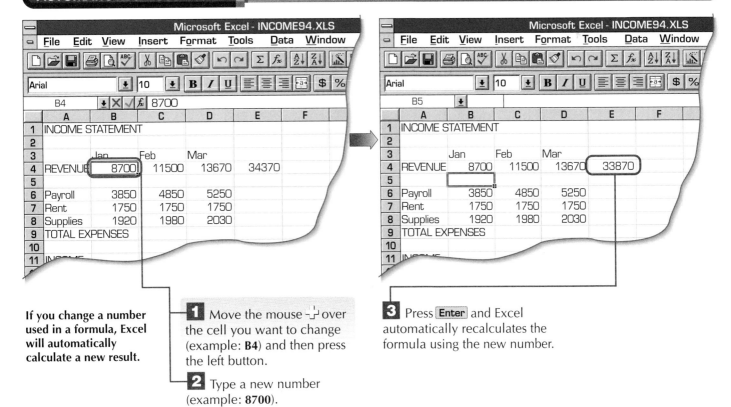

If you change a number used in a formula, Excel will automatically calculate a new result.

1 Move the mouse ⊹ over the cell you want to change (example: **B4**) and then press the left button.

2 Type a new number (example: **8700**).

3 Press **Enter** and Excel automatically recalculates the formula using the new number.

FUNCTIONS

A function is a ready-to-use formula. Excel offers over 300 functions to perform calculations on data in your worksheet.

You must tell Excel what data to use to calculate a function. This data is enclosed in parentheses ( ).

=SUM(A1,A3,A5)

◆ When there is a comma (,) between cell references in a function, Excel uses each cell to perform the calculation.

Example: =SUM(A1,A3,A5) is the same as the formula =A1+A3+A5.

=SUM(A1:A4)

◆ When there is a colon (:) between cell references in a function, Excel uses the displayed cells and all cells between them to perform the calculation.

Example: =SUM(A1:A4) is the same as the formula =A1+A2+A3+A4.

INTRODUCTION TO EXCEL

| Getting Started | Save and Open Your Workbooks | Edit Your Worksheets | **Using Formulas and Functions** | Working with Rows and Columns | Format Your Worksheets | Smart Formatting | Print Your Worksheets |

- Formulas
- Enter a Formula
- **Functions**
- Enter a Function
- Add Numbers
- Errors in Formulas
- Copy Formulas
- Name Cells

Common Functions

AVERAGE Calculates the average value of a list of numbers.
Example: =AVERAGE(B1:B6)

MIN Finds the smallest value in a list of numbers.
Example: =MIN(B1:B6)

COUNT Counts the number of values in a list of numbers.
Example: =COUNT(B1:B6)

ROUND Rounds a number to a specific number of digits.
Example: =ROUND(B6,2)

MAX Finds the largest value in a list of numbers.
Example: =MAX(B1:B6)

SUM Adds a list of numbers.
Example: =SUM(B1:B6)

◆ A function starts with an equal sign (=).

◆ You should use cell references (example: **A1**) instead of actual numbers whenever possible. This way, if your data changes, Excel will automatically redo the calculations.

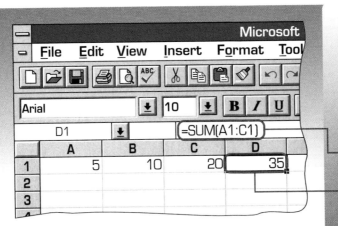

In this example, cell **D1** contains the function:

=SUM(A1:C1)

=A1+B1+C1

=5+10+20

=35

◆ The function for the active cell appears in the formula bar.

◆ The result of the calculation appears in the cell containing the function (example: **D1**).

ENTER A FUNCTION

The Function Wizard lets you perform calculations without typing long, complex formulas.

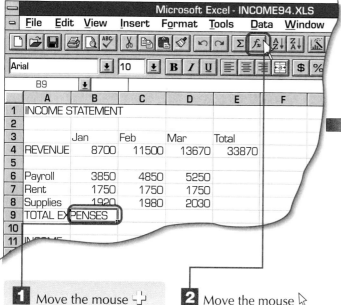

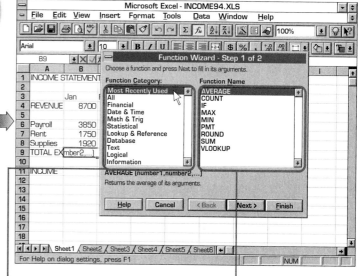

1 Move the mouse ⊹ over the cell where you want to enter a function (example: **B9**) and then press the left button.

2 Move the mouse ↖ over *fx* and then press the left button.

◆ The **Function Wizard** dialog box appears.

3 Move the mouse ↖ over the category containing the function you want to use and then press the left button.

*Note: If you do not know which category contains the function you want to use, select **All**. This will display a list of all the functions.*

◆ This area displays the functions in the category you selected.

Getting Started	Save and Open Your Workbooks	Edit Your Worksheets	**Using Formulas and Functions**	Working with Rows and Columns	Format Your Worksheets	Smart Formatting	Print Your Worksheets

- Formulas
- Enter a Formula
- Functions
- **Enter a Function**

- Add Numbers
- Errors in Formulas
- Copy Formulas
- Name Cells

Text
Logical
Information

SUM(number1,number2,...)

Adds its arguments.

| Help | Cancel | < Back |

◆ *Arguments are numbers in your worksheet that are used to calculate a function.*

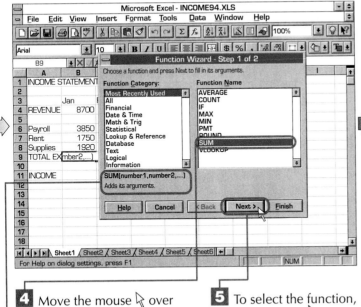

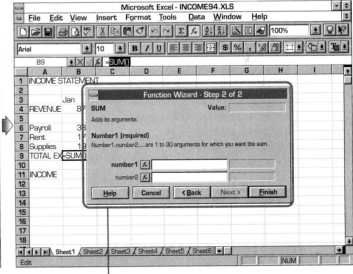

4 Move the mouse ⟍ over the function you want to use (example: **SUM**) and then press the left button.

◆ A description of the function you selected appears.

5 To select the function, move the mouse ⟍ over **Next** and then press the left button.

◆ This dialog box appears. The text in the dialog box depends on the function you selected in step **4**.

Note: To continue entering the function, refer to the next page.

63

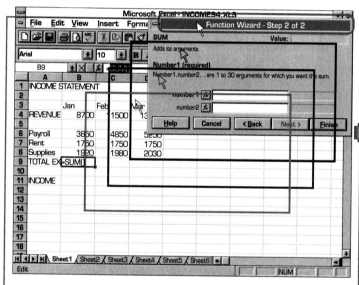

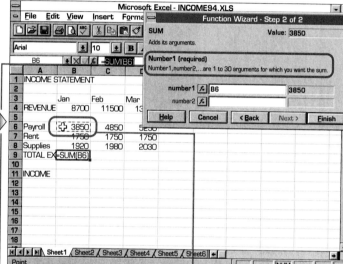

◆ If the **Function Wizard** dialog box covers data you want to use in the function, you can move it to another location on your screen.

6 To move the dialog box, position the mouse ⇖ over its title bar and then press and hold down the left button.

7 Still holding down the button, drag the box to a new location.

8 Release the button and the dialog box moves to the new location.

◆ This area describes the first number Excel needs to perform the function.

9 To select a number, move the mouse ⬚ over the cell containing the data you want to use and then press the left button.

Note: If the number you want to enter does not appear in your worksheet, type the number.

10 To display a description of the next number Excel needs to perform the function, press **Tab**.

Getting
Started

Save and
Open Your
Workbooks

Edit Your
Worksheets

**Using
Formulas
and Functions**

Working with
Rows and
Columns

Format Your
Worksheets

Smart
Formatting

Print Your
Worksheets

• Formulas
• Enter a Formula
• Functions
• **Enter a Function**

• Add Numbers
• Errors in Formulas
• Copy Formulas
• Name Cells

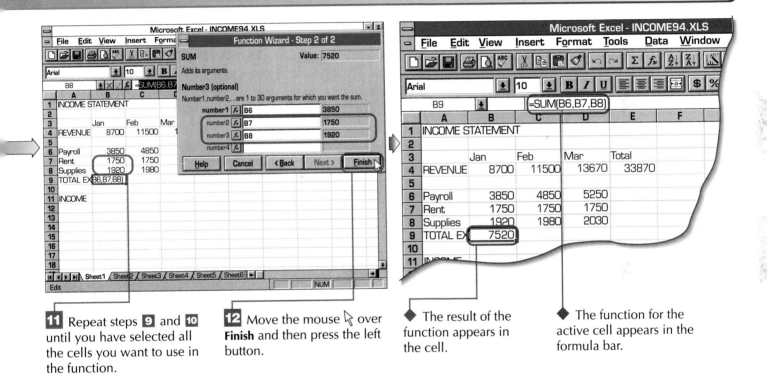

11 Repeat steps **9** and **10** until you have selected all the cells you want to use in the function.

12 Move the mouse ⤵ over **Finish** and then press the left button.

◆ The result of the function appears in the cell.

◆ The function for the active cell appears in the formula bar.

Tip

◆ In the above example, you can quickly enter numbers in the **Function Wizard** dialog box. Replace steps **9** to **11** by selecting cells **B6** to **B8**.

Note: To select cells, refer to page 12.

ADD NUMBERS

You can use the AutoSum feature to quickly add a list of numbers in your worksheet.

ADD A LIST OF NUMBERS

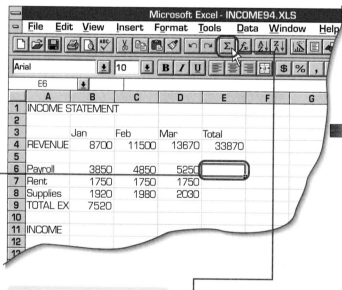

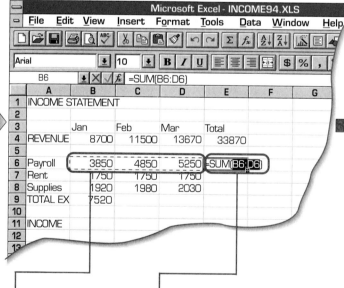

1 Move the mouse ✛ over the cell you want to display the sum (example: **E6**) and then press the left button.

2 Move the mouse ⬉ over Σ and then press the left button.

Note: Σ is the Greek symbol for sum.

◆ A moving border appears around the cells Excel will add together.

◆ The SUM function appears displaying the first and last cells Excel will add together, separated by a colon (:).

◆ To add a different list of cells, select the cells.

Note: To select cells, refer to page 12.

INTRODUCTION TO EXCEL

| Getting Started | Save and Open Your Workbooks | Edit Your Worksheets | **Using Formulas and Functions** | Working with Rows and Columns | Format Your Worksheets | Smart Formatting | Print Your Worksheets |

- Formulas
- Enter a Formula
- Functions
- Enter a Function

- **Add Numbers**
- Errors in Formulas
- Copy Formulas
- Name Cells

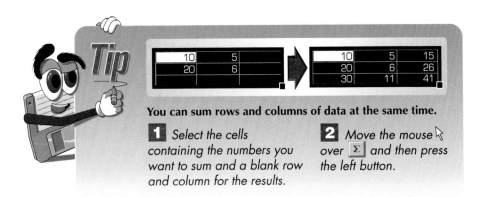

You can sum rows and columns of data at the same time.

1 *Select the cells containing the numbers you want to sum and a blank row and column for the results.*

2 *Move the mouse over* Σ *and then press the left button.*

ADD SEVERAL LISTS OF NUMBERS

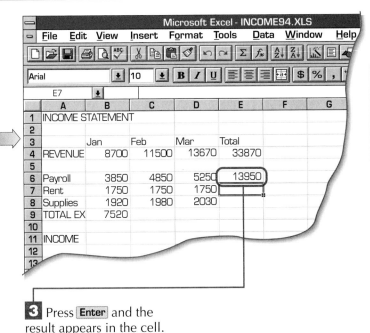

3 Press **Enter** and the result appears in the cell.

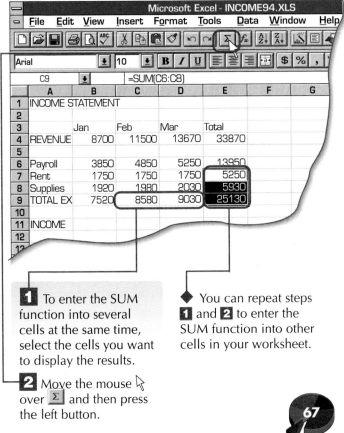

1 To enter the SUM function into several cells at the same time, select the cells you want to display the results.

2 Move the mouse over Σ and then press the left button.

◆ You can repeat steps **1** and **2** to enter the SUM function into other cells in your worksheet.

ERRORS IN FORMULAS

An error message appears when Excel cannot properly calculate a formula. You can correct an error by editing the cell displaying the error message.

COMMON ERRORS IN FORMULAS

#DIV/0!

This error appears in a cell if the formula you entered divides a number by zero.

	A	B	C	D
1	50		35	
2	0			
3	#DIV/0!		#DIV/0!	
4				
5				

This cell contains the formula =A1/A2 =50/0

The formula divides a number by 0.

This cell contains the formula =C1/C2 =35/0

The formula divides a number by 0.

Note: Excel considers a blank cell to contain the zero value.

#NAME?

This error appears in a cell if the formula you entered contains a name that Excel does not recognize.

	A	B	C	D
1	5		30	
2	10		5	
3	20		10	
4	#NAME?		#NAME?	
5				

This cell contains the formula =A1+A2A3

The formula is missing a plus sign (+).

This cell contains the function =SUMM(C1:C3)

The name of the function is misspelled.

68

INTRODUCTION TO EXCEL

| Getting Started | Save and Open Your Workbooks | Edit Your Worksheets | Using Formulas and Functions | Working with Rows and Columns | Format Your Worksheets | Smart Formatting | Print Your Worksheets |

- Formulas
- Enter a Formula
- Functions
- Enter a Function

- Add Numbers
- **Errors in Formulas**
- Copy Formulas
- Name Cells

CORRECT AN ERROR

1 To correct an error, move the mouse ⊕ over the cell displaying the error message and then quickly press the left button twice.

2 Correct the error by editing the formula as you would any data in your worksheet.

Note: To edit data, refer to page 40.

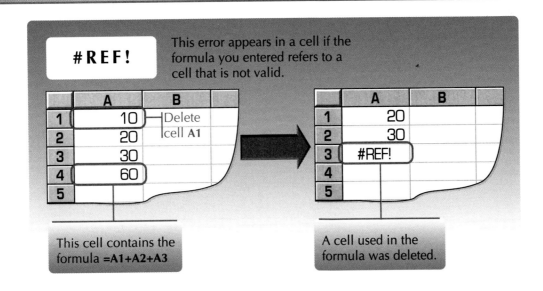

#REF!

This error appears in a cell if the formula you entered refers to a cell that is not valid.

This cell contains the formula =A1+A2+A3

A cell used in the formula was deleted.

COPY FORMULAS

After entering a formula in your worksheet, you can copy the formula to other cells.

COPY FORMULAS (USING RELATIVE REFERENCES)

1 Type and enter the formula you want to copy to other cells (example: **=B4-B9** in cell **B11** to calculate INCOME).

2 Move the mouse ⇧ over the cell containing the formula (example: **B11**) and then press the left button.

3 Move the mouse ⇧ over the bottom right corner of the cell and ⇧ changes to **+**.

4 Press and hold down the left button as you drag the mouse **+** over the cells you want to receive a copy of the formula.

| Getting Started | Save and Open Your Workbooks | Edit Your Worksheets | Using Formulas and Functions | Working with Rows and Columns | Format Your Worksheets | Smart Formatting | Print Your Worksheets |

- Formulas
- Enter a Formula
- Functions
- Enter a Function

- Add Numbers
- Errors in Formulas
- **Copy Formulas**
- Name Cells

When you copy a formula, Excel automatically changes the cell references in the formula.

	A	B	C	
1	10	20	5	
2	20	30	10	
3	30	40	20	
4	60	90	35	
5				
6				
7				

=A1+A2+A3 ➡ =B1+B2+B3   =C1+C2+C3

This cell contains the formula =A1+A2+A3

If you copy the formula to other cells in the worksheet, the cell references in the new formulas automatically change.

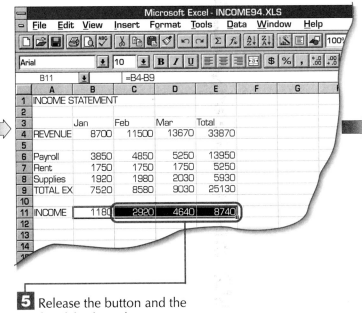

5 Release the button and the results of the formulas appear.

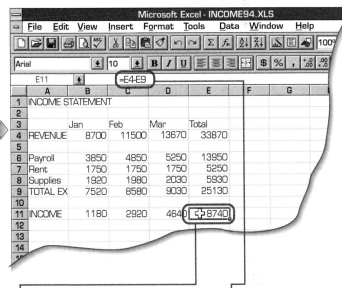

6 To see how the cell references changed, move the mouse over a cell that received a copy of the formula (example: **E11**) and then press the left button.

◆ The cell references in the formula changed.

COPY FORMULAS

You can copy a formula to other cells in your worksheet. If you do not want Excel to change a cell reference, you must lock the reference when copying the formula. A locked cell reference is called an absolute reference.

COPY FORMULAS (USING ABSOLUTE REFERENCES)

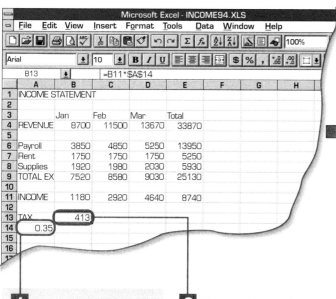

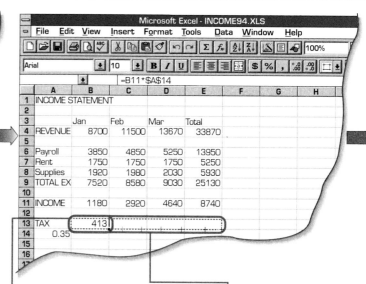

1 Type and enter the data you want to use as an absolute cell reference (example: **0.35** in cell **A14**).

2 Type and enter the formula you want to copy to other cells (example: **=B11*$A$14** in cell **B13**).

Note: To lock a cell reference during the copy process, type a dollar sign ($) before both the column letter and row number (example: $A$14).

3 Move the mouse ⊹ over the cell containing the formula you want to copy (example: **B13**) and then press the left button.

4 Move the mouse ⊹ over the bottom right corner of the cell and ⊹ changes to + .

5 Press and hold down the left button as you drag the mouse + over the cells you want to receive a copy of the formula.

INTRODUCTION TO EXCEL

| Getting Started | Save and Open Your Workbooks | Edit Your Worksheets | Using Formulas and Functions | Working with Rows and Columns | Format Your Worksheets | Smart Formatting | Print Your Worksheets |

- Formulas
- Enter a Formula
- Functions
- Enter a Function
- Add Numbers
- Errors in Formulas
- **Copy Formulas**
- Name Cells

To make a cell reference absolute, type a dollar sign ($) before both the column letter and row number (example: $B$1).

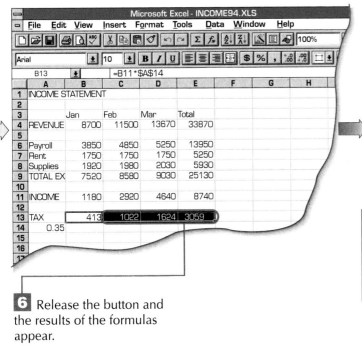

	A	B	C	D	E
1	Cost per Item	$10			
2					
3	Number of Items	10	20	30	
4	Total Cost	$100	$200	$300	
5					
6					
7					

=$B$1*B3 → =$B$1*C3   =$B$1*D3

This cell contains the formula =$B$1*B3

If you copy the formula to other cells in the worksheet, the cell reference B1 does not change in the new formulas.

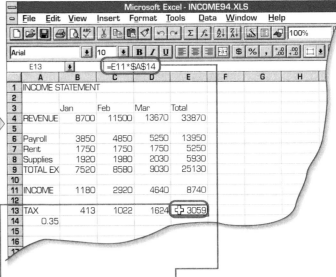

6 Release the button and the results of the formulas appear.

7 To see how the cell references changed, move the mouse over a cell that received a copy of the formula (example: **E13**) and then press the left button.

◆ The absolute reference in the formula did not change (example: **A14**). The relative reference in the formula did change (example: **E11**).

NAME CELLS

You can save time by using names to refer to cells in your worksheet.

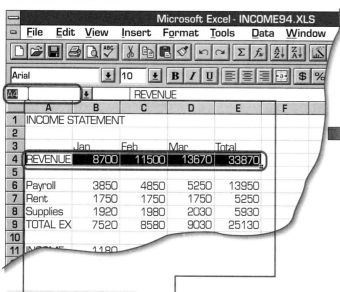

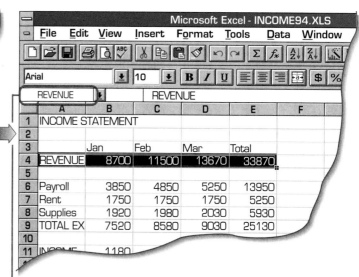

1 Select the cells you want to name.

Note: To select cells, refer to page 12.

2 Move the mouse I over the **Name** box and then press the left button.

3 Type a name for the cells (example: **REVENUE**).

Note: The name must begin with a letter and cannot contain any spaces.

4 Press Enter on your keyboard.

Note: To deselect the cells, move the mouse over any cell in your worksheet and then press the left button.

| Getting Started | Save and Open Your Workbooks | Edit Your Worksheets | Using Formulas and Functions | Working with Rows and Columns | Format Your Worksheets | Smart Formatting | Print Your Worksheets |

- Formulas
- Enter a Formula
- Functions
- Enter a Function
- Add Numbers
- Errors in Formulas
- Copy Formulas
- **Name Cells**

Named cells make formulas easier to understand.

	A	B	
1	Revenue	$8,700	
2	Expenses	$7,520	
3	Income	$1,180	
4			

◆ In this example:
Cell **B1** is named **Revenue**.
Cell **B2** is named **Expenses**.
Cell **B3** contains the formula: **=Revenue-Expenses**.
This formula is easier to understand than the formula **=B1-B2** because it contains names instead of cell references.

SELECT NAMED CELLS

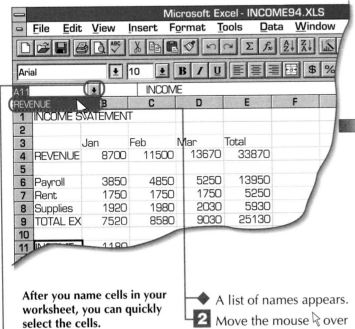

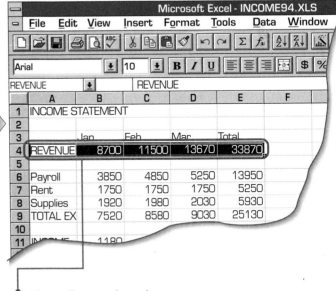

After you name cells in your worksheet, you can quickly select the cells.

1 Move the mouse over ⬇ beside the **Name** box and then press the left button.

◆ A list of names appears.

2 Move the mouse over the name of the cells you want to select and then press the left button.

◆ The cells are selected.

verview

WORKING WITH ROWS AND COLUMNS

Insert a Row or Column

Delete a Row or Column

Change Column Width

Change Row Height

◆ In this chapter, you will learn to add, delete and adjust the rows and columns in your worksheet.

INSERT A ROW OR COLUMN

You can add a row or column to your worksheet if you want to insert new data.

INSERT A ROW

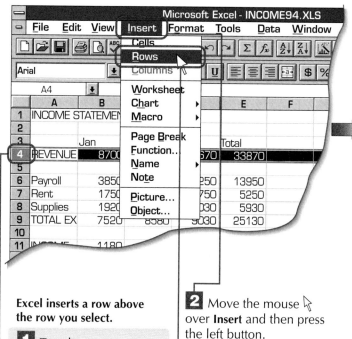

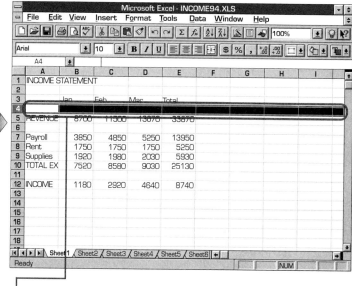

Excel inserts a row above the row you select.

1 To select a row, move the mouse ⊕ over the row heading (example: **row 4**) and then press the left button.

2 Move the mouse ⊳ over **Insert** and then press the left button.

3 Move the mouse ⊳ over **Rows** and then press the left button.

◆ The new row appears and all the rows that follow shift downward.

INTRODUCTION TO EXCEL

| Getting Started | Save and Open Your Workbooks | Edit Your Worksheets | Using Formulas and Functions | Working with Rows and Columns | Format Your Worksheets | Smart Formatting | Print Your Worksheets |

• **Insert a Row or Column**
• Delete a Row or Column
• Change Column Width
• Change Row Height

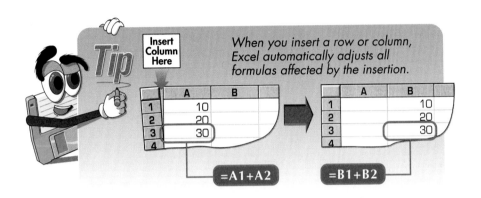

Tip

When you insert a row or column, Excel automatically adjusts all formulas affected by the insertion.

=A1+A2 → =B1+B2

INSERT A COLUMN

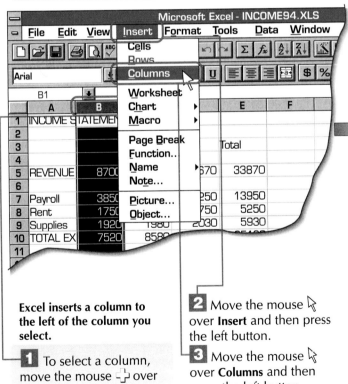

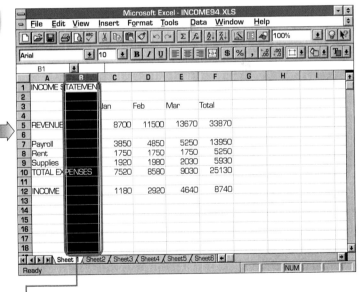

Excel inserts a column to the left of the column you select.

1 To select a column, move the mouse ⇩ over the column heading (example: **column B**) and then press the left button.

2 Move the mouse ⇩ over **Insert** and then press the left button.

3 Move the mouse ⇩ over **Columns** and then press the left button.

◆ The new column appears and all the columns that follow shift to the right.

DELETE A ROW OR COLUMN

> You can delete a row or column from your worksheet. This lets you remove cells you no longer need.

DELETE A ROW

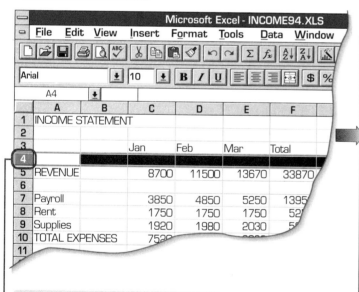

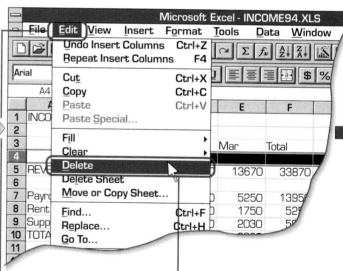

1 To select the row you want to delete, move the mouse ⊕ over the row heading (example: **row 4**) and then press the left button.

2 Move the mouse ⍦ over **Edit** and then press the left button.

3 Move the mouse ⍦ over **Delete** and then press the left button.

INTRODUCTION TO EXCEL

Getting Started	Save and Open Your Workbooks	Edit Your Worksheets	Using Formulas and Functions	Working with Rows and Columns	Format Your Worksheets	Smart Formatting	Print Your Worksheets

- Insert a Row or Column
- **Delete a Row or Column**
- Change Column Width
- Change Row Height

Tip

#REF!

If #REF! appears in a cell in your worksheet, you have deleted data needed to calculate a formula.

1 *To immediately cancel the deletion, move the mouse ⅄ over ⟲ and then press the left button.*

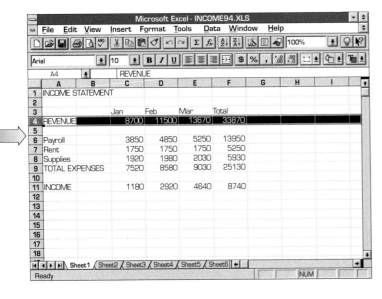

◆ The row disappears and all the rows that follow shift upward.

DELETE A COLUMN

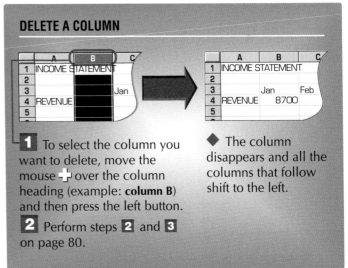

1 To select the column you want to delete, move the mouse ✛ over the column heading (example: **column B**) and then press the left button.

2 Perform steps **2** and **3** on page 80.

◆ The column disappears and all the columns that follow shift to the left.

CHANGE COLUMN WIDTH

You can improve the appearance of your worksheet and display hidden data by changing the width of columns.

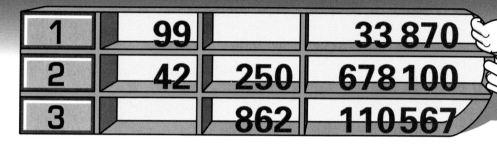

CHANGE COLUMN WIDTH

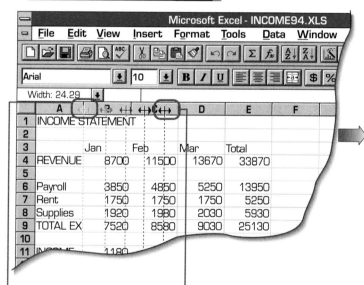

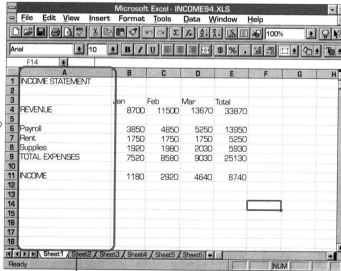

1 Move the mouse ⟐ over the right edge of the column heading you want to change (example: **column A**) and ⟐ changes to ↔ .

2 Press and hold down the left button as you drag the edge of the column to a new position.

◆ A dotted line indicates the new column width.

3 Release the button and the new column width appears.

| Getting Started | Save and Open Your Workbooks | Edit Your Worksheets | Using Formulas and Functions | Working with Rows and Columns | Format Your Worksheets | Smart Formatting | Print Your Worksheets |

Working with Rows and Columns
- Insert a Row or Column
- Delete a Row or Column
- **Change Column Width**
- Change Row Height

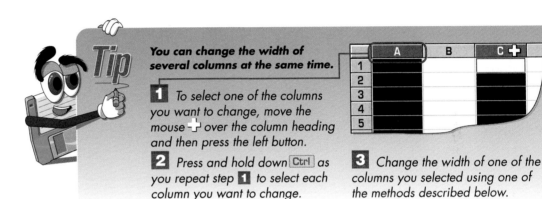

You can change the width of several columns at the same time.

1 To select one of the columns you want to change, move the mouse ✛ over the column heading and then press the left button.

2 Press and hold down `Ctrl` as you repeat step **1** to select each column you want to change.

3 Change the width of one of the columns you selected using one of the methods described below.

CHANGE COLUMN WIDTH AUTOMATICALLY

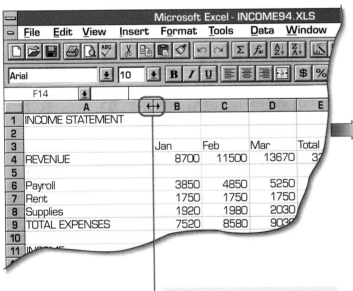

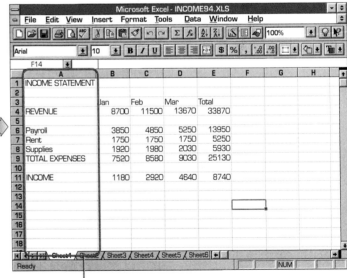

You can have Excel adjust the column width to fit the longest item in the column.

1 Move the mouse ✛ over the right edge of the column heading you want to change (example: **column A**) and ✛ changes to ↔.

2 Quickly press the left button twice.

◆ The column width changes to fit the longest item in the column.

83

CHANGE ROW HEIGHT

You can change the height of a row. This lets you display a title at the top of your worksheet or add space between rows of data.

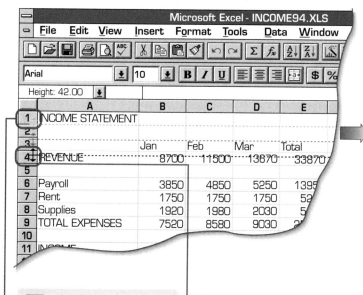

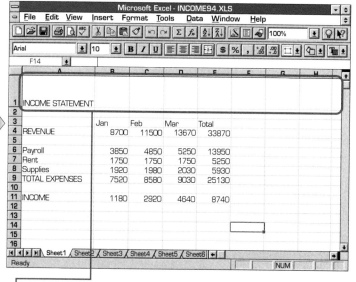

1 Move the mouse ⬚ over the bottom edge of the row heading you want to change (example: **row 1**) and ⬚ changes to ↕ .

2 Press and hold down the left button as you drag the edge of the row to a new position.

◆ A dotted line indicates the new row height.

3 Release the button and the new row height appears.

84

| Getting Started | Save and Open Your Workbooks | Edit Your Worksheets | Using Formulas and Functions | Working with Rows and Columns | Format Your Worksheets | Smart Formatting | Print Your Worksheets |

Working with Rows and Columns
- Insert a Row or Column
- Delete a Row or Column
- Change Column Width
- **Change Row Height**

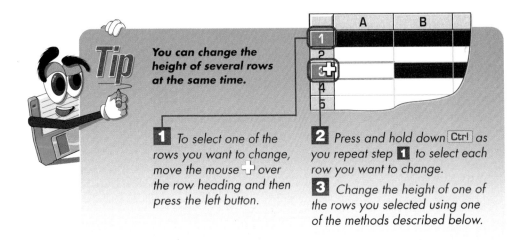

You can change the height of several rows at the same time.

1 To select one of the rows you want to change, move the mouse ⊹ over the row heading and then press the left button.

2 Press and hold down Ctrl as you repeat step **1** to select each row you want to change.

3 Change the height of one of the rows you selected using one of the methods described below.

CHANGE ROW HEIGHT AUTOMATICALLY

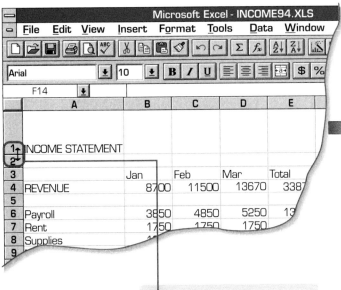

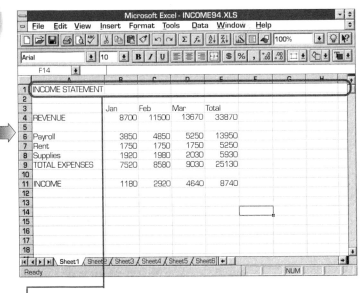

You can have Excel adjust the row height to fit the tallest item in the row.

1 Move the mouse ⊹ over the bottom edge of the row heading you want to change (example: **row 1**) and ⊹ changes to ↕.

2 Quickly press the left button twice.

◆ The row height changes to fit the tallest item in the row.

Overview

FORMAT YOUR WORKSHEETS

Change Appearance of Numbers

Align Data

Center Data Across Columns

Bold, Italic and Underline

Clear Formats

Change Fonts

Change Data Orientation

Add Borders

Add Color

◆ In this chapter, you will learn how to change the appearance of data in your worksheet.

CHANGE APPEARANCE OF NUMBERS

You can change the appearance of numbers in your worksheet without having to retype them. This can make the numbers easier to understand.

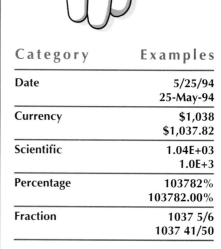

Category	Examples
Date	5/25/94
	25-May-94
Currency	$1,038
	$1,037.82
Scientific	1.04E+03
	1.0E+3
Percentage	103782%
	103782.00%
Fraction	1037 5/6
	1037 41/50

CHANGE APPEARANCE OF NUMBERS

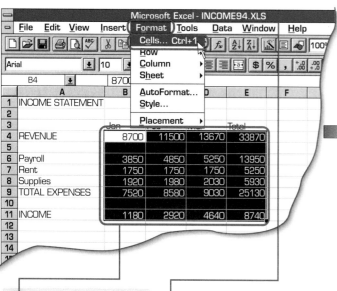

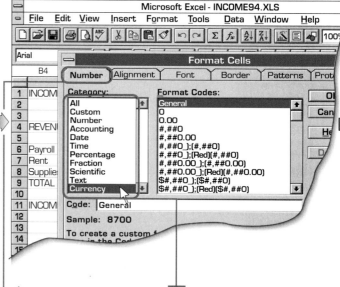

1 Select the cells containing the numbers you want to change.

Note: To select cells, refer to page 12.

2 Move the mouse over **Format** and then press the left button.

3 Move the mouse over **Cells** and then press the left button.

◆ The **Format Cells** dialog box appears.

4 Move the mouse over the **Number** tab and then press the left button.

5 Move the mouse over the category that contains the number style you want to use (example: **Currency**) and then press the left button.

*Note: If you do not know which category contains the style you want to use, select **All**. This will display a list of all the styles.*

| Getting Started | Save and Open Your Workbooks | Edit Your Worksheets | Using Formulas and Functions | Working with Rows and Columns | **Format Your Worksheets** | Smart Formatting | Print Your Worksheets |

- **Change Appearance of Numbers**
- Align Data
- Center Data Across Columns
- Bold, Italic and Underline
- Clear Formats
- Change Fonts
- Change Data Orientation
- Add Borders
- Add Color

SHORTCUT

To quickly change the appearance of numbers in your worksheet:

1 Select the cells containing the numbers you want to change.

2 Move the mouse ⌖ over one of the following options and then press the left button.

$ Displays the number as a dollar value. Example: 7147 ➔ $7,147.00

% Displays the number as a percentage. Example: 0.35 ➔ 35%

, Adds a comma and two decimal places to the number. Example: 2683 ➔ 2,683.00

.00 Adds one decimal place to the number. Example: 52.3 ➔ 52.30

.00 Deletes one decimal place from the number. Example: 49.27 ➔ 49.3

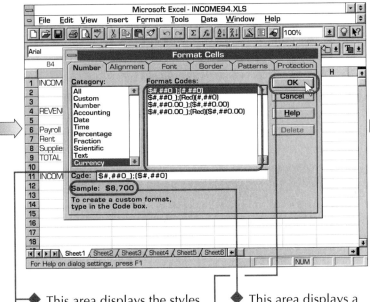

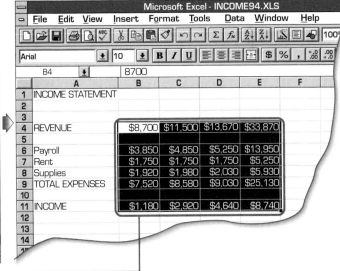

◆ This area displays the styles in the category you selected.

6 Move the mouse ⌖ over the style you want to use and then press the left button.

◆ This area displays a sample of the style you selected.

7 Move the mouse ⌖ over **OK** and then press the left button.

◆ The numbers in the cells you selected display the new style.

Note: If number signs (#) appear in a cell, the column is not wide enough to display the entire number. To change the column width, refer to page 82.

ALIGN DATA

CENTER DATA ACROSS COLUMNS

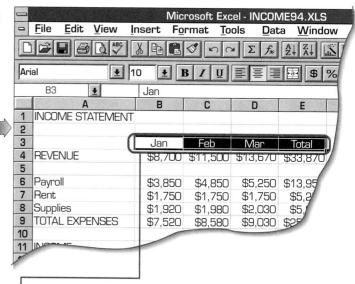

You can change the position of data in each cell of your worksheet. Excel offers several alignment options.

Data	**Left Align**
Data	**Center**
Data	**Right Align**

ALIGN DATA

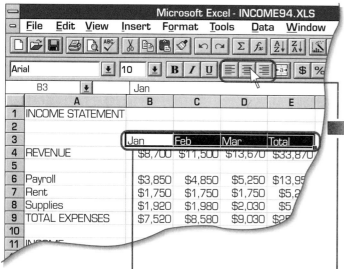

1 Select the cells containing the data you want to align.

Note: To select cells, refer to page 12.

2 Move the mouse ℝ over one of the options listed below and then press the left button.

⬛ Left align data

⬛ Center data

⬛ Right align data

◆ The data in the cells you selected displays the new alignment.

Note: In this example, the data appears centered in the cells.

Getting Started	Save and Open Your Workbooks	Edit Your Worksheets	Using Formulas and Functions	Working with Rows and Columns	Format Your Worksheets	Smart Formatting	Print Your Worksheets

- Change Appearance of Numbers
- **Align Data**
- **Center Data Across Columns**
- Bold, Italic and Underline
- Clear Formats

- Change Fonts
- Change Data Orientation
- Add Borders
- Add Color

You can center data across columns in your worksheet. This is useful for displaying titles.

CENTER DATA ACROSS COLUMNS

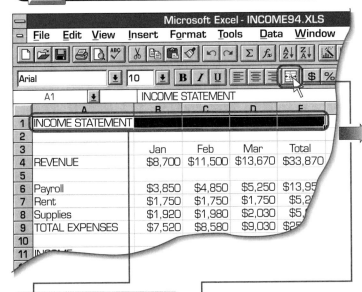

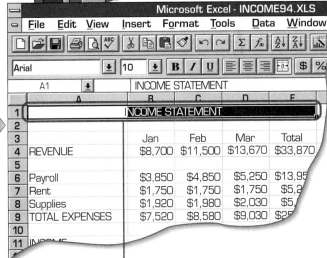

1 To center data across columns, select the cells you want to center the data between.

Note: For best results, the first cell you select should contain the data you want to center.

2 Move the mouse over ⊞ and then press the left button.

◆ Excel displays the data centered between the cells you selected.

91

BOLD, ITALIC AND UNDERLINE

CLEAR FORMATS

You can use the Bold, Italic and Underline features to emphasize important data. This will improve the overall appearance of your worksheet.

bold *italic* <u>underline</u>

B I U — BOLD, ITALIC AND UNDERLINE

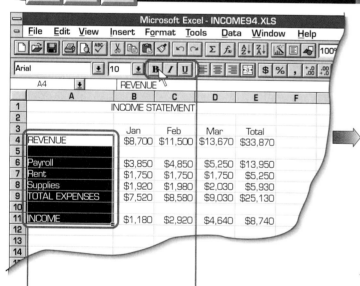

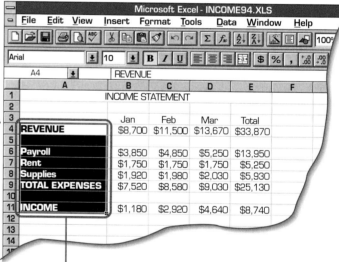

1 Select the cells containing the data you want to change.

Note: To select cells, refer to page 12.

2 Move the mouse ℟ over one of the following options and then press the left button.

B Bold data

I Italicize data

U Underline data

♦ The data in the cells you selected appears in the new style.

Note: In this example, the data appears in the bold style.

Remove Bold, Italic or Underline

Repeat steps **1** and **2**.

92

Getting Started	Save and Open Your Workbooks	Edit Your Worksheets	Using Formulas and Functions	Working with Rows and Columns	**Format Your Worksheets**	Smart Formatting	Print Your Worksheets

- Change Appearance of Numbers
- Align Data
- Center Data Across Columns
- **Bold, Italic and Underline**
- **Clear Formats**

- Change Fonts
- Change Data Orientation
- Add Borders
- Add Color

If you have applied several formats to cells in your worksheet, you can quickly remove all the formatting at once.

CLEAR FORMATS

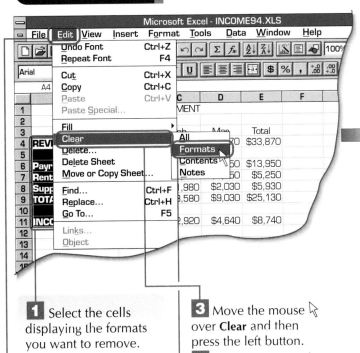

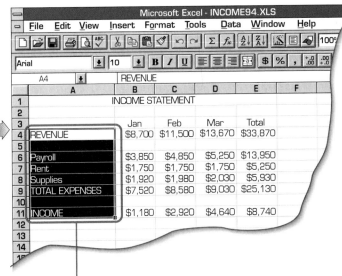

1 Select the cells displaying the formats you want to remove.

Note: To select cells, refer to page 12.

2 Move the mouse over **Edit** and then press the left button.

3 Move the mouse over **Clear** and then press the left button.

4 Move the mouse over **Formats** and then press the left button.

◆ All formats disappear from the cells you selected. The data remains unchanged.

CHANGE FONTS

You can change the design and size of data in your worksheet to emphasize headings and make data easier to read.

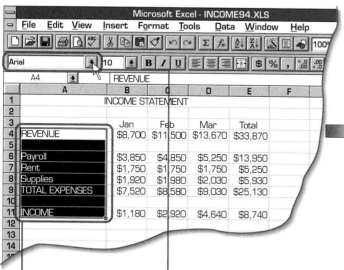

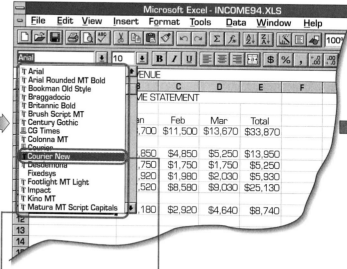

1 Select the cells containing the data you want to change to a new font.

Note: To select cells, refer to page 12.

◆ The **Font** box displays the font of the active cell (example: **Arial**).

2 To display a list of the available fonts, move the mouse �️ over ⬇️ beside the **Font** box and then press the left button.

◆ A list of the available fonts for your computer appears.

3 Press ⬇️ or ⬆️ on your keyboard until you highlight the font you want to use (example: **Courier New**).

4 To select the highlighted font, press **Enter**.

| Getting Started | Save and Open Your Workbooks | Edit Your Worksheets | Using Formulas and Functions | Working with Rows and Columns | **Format Your Worksheets** | Smart Formatting | Print Your Worksheets |

• Change Appearance of Numbers
• Align Data
• Center Data Across Columns
• Bold, Italic and Underline
• Clear Formats

• **Change Fonts**
• Change Data Orientation
• Add Borders
• Add Color

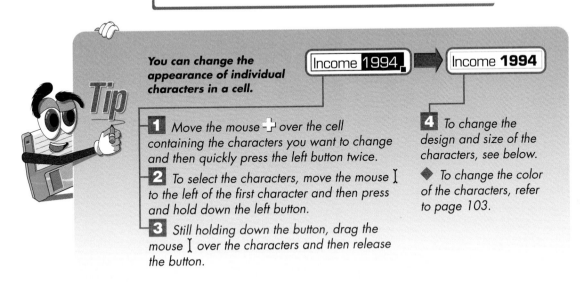

You can change the appearance of individual characters in a cell.

Income 1994 ➜ Income **1994**

1 Move the mouse ✚ over the cell containing the characters you want to change and then quickly press the left button twice.

2 To select the characters, move the mouse I to the left of the first character and then press and hold down the left button.

3 Still holding down the button, drag the mouse I over the characters and then release the button.

4 To change the design and size of the characters, see below.

◆ To change the color of the characters, refer to page 103.

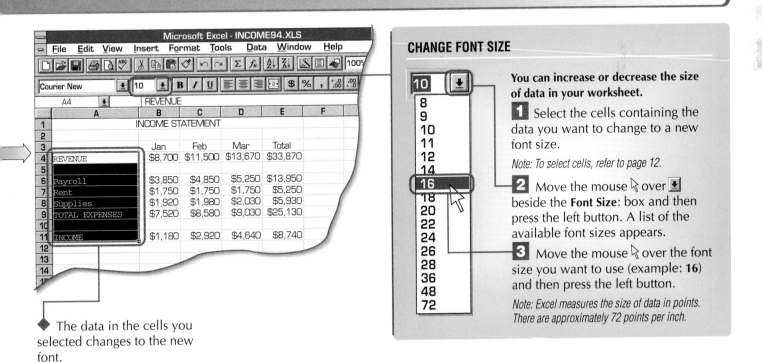

CHANGE FONT SIZE

You can increase or decrease the size of data in your worksheet.

1 Select the cells containing the data you want to change to a new font size.

Note: To select cells, refer to page 12.

2 Move the mouse ⌖ over ⯆ beside the **Font Size:** box and then press the left button. A list of the available font sizes appears.

3 Move the mouse ⌖ over the font size you want to use (example: **16**) and then press the left button.

Note: Excel measures the size of data in points. There are approximately 72 points per inch.

◆ The data in the cells you selected changes to the new font.

You can change the design and size of data in your worksheet at the same time by using the Format Cells dialog box.

CHANGE FONTS

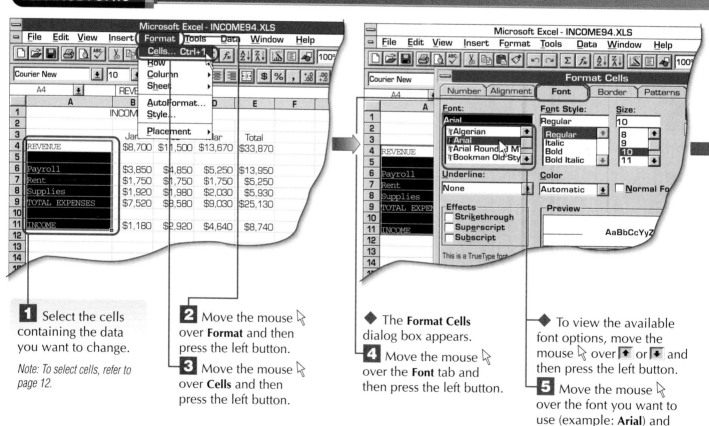

1 Select the cells containing the data you want to change.

Note: To select cells, refer to page 12.

2 Move the mouse over **Format** and then press the left button.

3 Move the mouse over **Cells** and then press the left button.

◆ The **Format Cells** dialog box appears.

4 Move the mouse over the **Font** tab and then press the left button.

◆ To view the available font options, move the mouse over ⬆ or ⬇ and then press the left button.

5 Move the mouse over the font you want to use (example: **Arial**) and then press the left button.

| Getting Started | Save and Open Your Workbooks | Edit Your Worksheets | Using Formulas and Functions | Working with Rows and Columns | **Format Your Worksheets** | Smart Formatting | Print Your Worksheets |

- Change Appearance of Numbers
- Align Data
- Center Data Across Columns
- Bold, Italic and Underline
- Clear Formats

- **Change Fonts**
- Change Data Orientation
- Add Borders
- Add Color

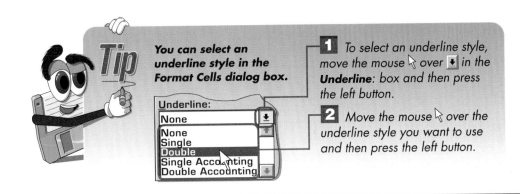

You can select an underline style in the Format Cells dialog box.

1 To select an underline style, move the mouse over ↓ in the **Underline:** box and then press the left button.

2 Move the mouse over the underline style you want to use and then press the left button.

Underline:
None
None
Single
Double
Single Accounting
Double Accounting

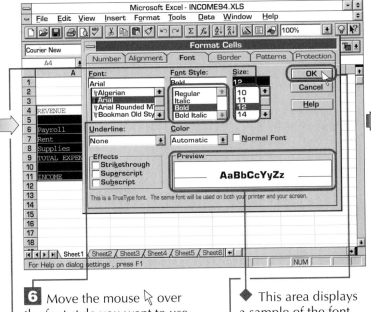

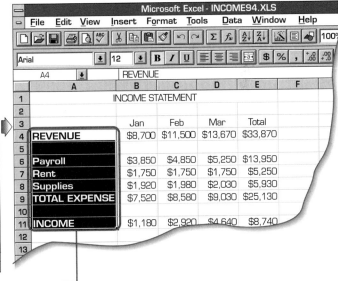

6 Move the mouse over the font style you want to use (example: **Bold**) and then press the left button.

7 Move the mouse over the font size you want to use (example: **12**) and then press the left button.

*Note: To select an underline style, see the **Tip** above.*

◆ This area displays a sample of the font you selected.

8 To confirm the changes, move the mouse over **OK** and then press the left button.

◆ The data in the cells you selected displays the font changes.

CHANGE DATA ORIENTATION

You can use Excel's Alignment feature to rotate data in your worksheet.

CHANGE DATA ORIENTATION

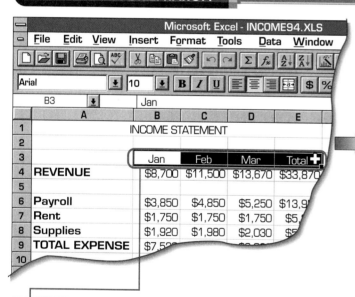

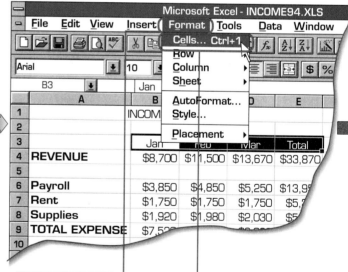

1 Select the cells containing the data you want to change.

Note: To select cells, refer to page 12.

2 Move the mouse ⤢ over **Format** and then press the left button.

3 Move the mouse ⤢ over **Cells** and then press the left button.

Getting Started	Save and Open Your Workbooks	Edit Your Worksheets	Using Formulas and Functions	Working with Rows and Columns	Format Your Worksheets	Smart Formatting	Print Your Worksheets

• Change Appearance of Numbers
• Align Data
• Center Data Across Columns
• Bold, Italic and Underline
• Clear Formats

• Change Fonts
• **Change Data Orientation**
• Add Borders
• Add Color

WRAP TEXT IN A CELL

Wrap text in a cell

⬇

Wrap text in a cell

You can fit a long line of text in one cell by wrapping the text.

1 Select the cell(s) containing the text you want to wrap.

Note: To select cells, refer to page 12.

2 Perform steps **2** to **4** starting on page 98.

3 Move the mouse ⇧ over **Wrap Text** and then press the left button (☐ becomes ⊠).

4 Move the mouse ⇧ over **OK** and then press the left button.

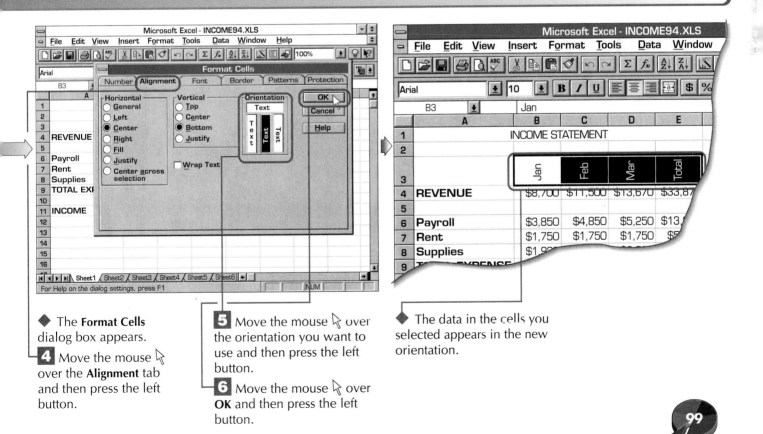

◆ The **Format Cells** dialog box appears.

4 Move the mouse ⇧ over the **Alignment** tab and then press the left button.

5 Move the mouse ⇧ over the orientation you want to use and then press the left button.

6 Move the mouse ⇧ over **OK** and then press the left button.

◆ The data in the cells you selected appears in the new orientation.

ADD BORDERS

You can add borders to draw attention to important data in your worksheet.

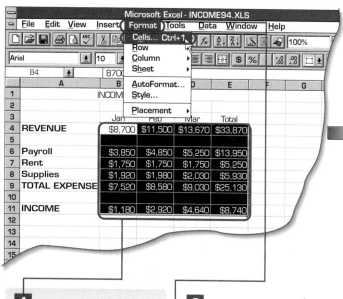

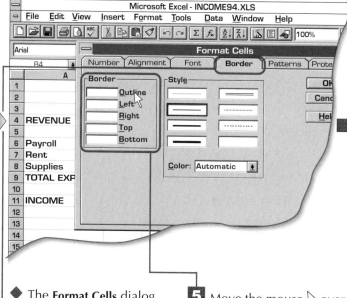

1 Select the cells you want to display borders.

Note: To select cells, refer to page 12.

2 Move the mouse over **Format** and then press the left button.

3 Move the mouse over **Cells** and then press the left button.

◆ The **Format Cells** dialog box appears.

4 Move the mouse over the **Border** tab and then press the left button.

5 Move the mouse over the border you want to add (example: **Outline**) and then press the left button.

| Getting Started | Save and Open Your Workbooks | Edit Your Worksheets | Using Formulas and Functions | Working with Rows and Columns | **Format Your Worksheets** | Smart Formatting | Print Your Worksheets |

- Change Appearance of Numbers
- Align Data
- Center Data Across Columns
- Bold, Italic and Underline
- Clear Formats

- Change Fonts
- Change Data Orientation
- **Add Borders**
- Add Color

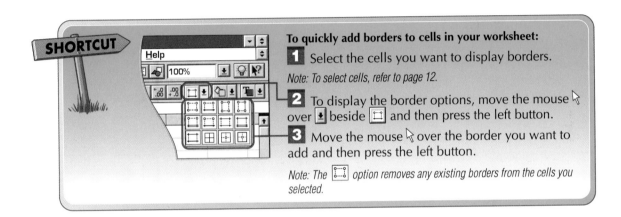

SHORTCUT

To quickly add borders to cells in your worksheet:

1 Select the cells you want to display borders.

Note: To select cells, refer to page 12.

2 To display the border options, move the mouse over ⏷ beside 🔲 and then press the left button.

3 Move the mouse over the border you want to add and then press the left button.

Note: The option removes any existing borders from the cells you selected.

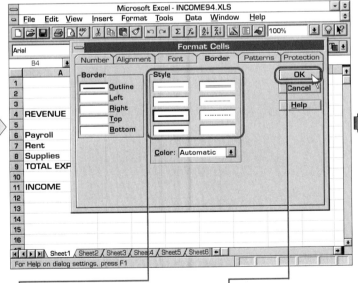

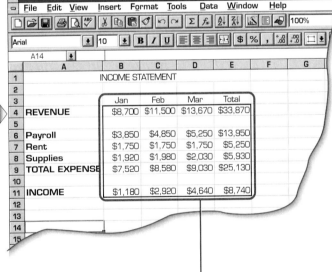

6 To select a line style for the border, move the mouse over the style and then press the left button.

7 Repeat steps **5** and **6** for each border you want to add.

8 Move the mouse over **OK** and then press the left button.

9 To view the borders, move the mouse outside the selected area and then press the left button.

◆ The cells display the borders.

ADD COLOR

Excel lets you add color to your worksheet. You can change the color of a cell or the data in a cell.

CHANGE CELL COLOR

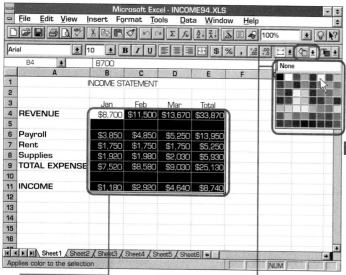

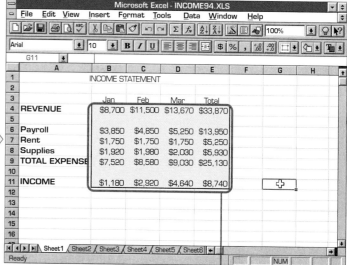

1 Select the cells you want to display color.

Note: To select cells, refer to page 12.

2 To display the color options, move the mouse over ▾ beside 🖫 and then press the left button.

3 Move the mouse over the color you want to add and then press the left button.

4 To view the new color, move the mouse outside the selected area and then press the left button.

◆ The cells display the color you selected.

102

| Getting Started | Save and Open Your Workbooks | Edit Your Worksheets | Using Formulas and Functions | Working with Rows and Columns | **Format Your Worksheets** | Smart Formatting | Print Your Worksheets |

- Change Appearance of Numbers
- Align Data
- Center Data Across Columns
- Bold, Italic and Underline
- Clear Formats

- Change Fonts
- Change Data Orientation
- Add Borders
- **Add Color**

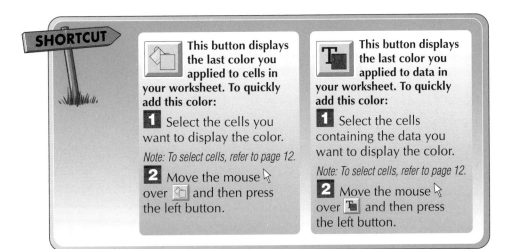

SHORTCUT

This button displays the last color you applied to cells in your worksheet. **To quickly add this color:**

1 Select the cells you want to display the color.

Note: To select cells, refer to page 12.

2 Move the mouse over 🖫 and then press the left button.

This button displays the last color you applied to data in your worksheet. **To quickly add this color:**

1 Select the cells containing the data you want to display the color.

Note: To select cells, refer to page 12.

2 Move the mouse over 🖫 and then press the left button.

CHANGE DATA COLOR

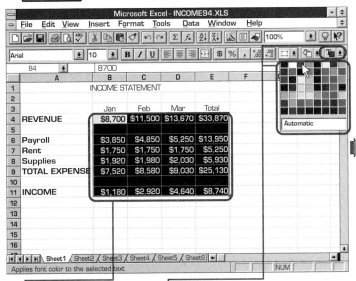

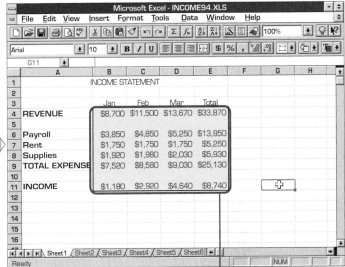

1 Select the cells containing the data you want to display color.

Note: To select cells, refer to page 12.

2 To display the color options, move the mouse over ⬇ beside 🖫 and then press the left button.

3 Move the mouse over the color you want to add and then press the left button.

4 To view the new color, move the mouse outside the selected area and then press the left button.

◆ The data in the cells displays the color you selected.

verview

SMART FORMATTING

Copy Formats

Create a Style

Apply a Style

Change an Existing Style

Format a Worksheet Automatically

◆ In this chapter you will learn time saving features to quickly change the appearance of cells in your worksheet.

COPY FORMATS

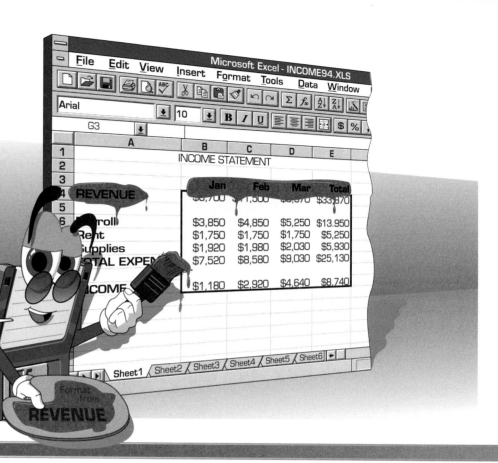

If you like the appearance of a cell in your worksheet, you can copy the formats to other cells.

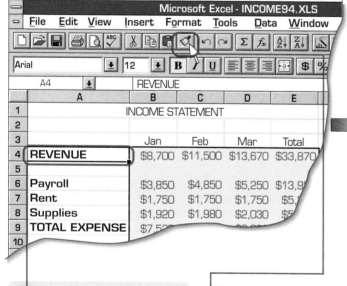

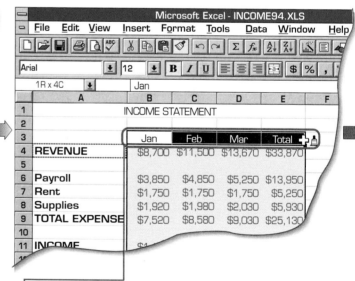

1 Move the mouse ⊹ over the cell displaying the formats you want to copy to other cells and then press the left button.

2 Move the mouse ⇗ over ◻ and then press the left button (⇗ changes to ⊹🖌).

3 Select the cells you want to display the formats.

Note: To select cells, refer to page 12.

INTRODUCTION TO EXCEL

| Getting Started | Save and Open Your Workbooks | Edit Your Worksheets | Using Formulas and Functions | Working with Rows and Columns | Format Your Worksheets | Smart Formatting | Print Your Worksheets |

- **Copy Formats**
- Create a Style
- Apply a Style
- Change an Existing Style
- Format a Worksheet Automatically

Tip

If you want to copy a set of formats to many parts of your worksheet, you can create a style. Excel will remember the formats so you can copy them at any time. For more information on styles, refer to page 108.

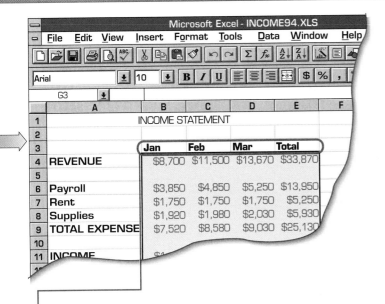

When you release the left button, the cells you selected display the new formats.

Note: To deselect cells, move the mouse over any cell in your worksheet and then press the left button.

You can copy formats to more than one location in your worksheet.

1 Move the mouse ➕ over the cell displaying the formats you want to copy to other cells and then press the left button.

2 Move the mouse ⬁ over 🖌 and then quickly press the left button twice (⬁ changes to ➕🖌).

3 Select the cells you want to display the formats.

4 Repeat step **3** until you have selected all the cells you want to display the formats.

5 When you finish copying the formats, press **Esc** on your keyboard.

CREATE A STYLE

A style is a set of commands that change the appearance of cells in your worksheet. If you frequently apply the same formats to parts of your worksheet, styles will save you time.

CREATE A STYLE

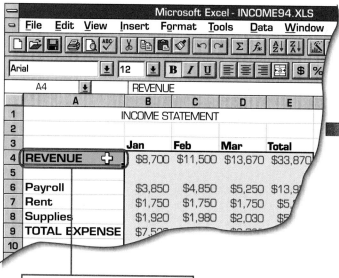

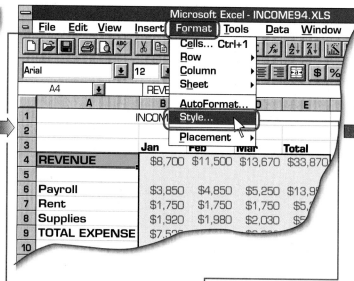

1 Format a cell with the characteristics you want to copy to other cells.

Note: To add color to a cell in your worksheet, refer to page 102.

2 To select the cell, move the mouse ⟱ over the cell and then press the left button.

3 Move the mouse ⟱ over **Format** and then press the left button.

4 Move the mouse ⟱ over **Style** and then press the left button.

INTRODUCTION TO EXCEL

| Getting Started | Save and Open Your Workbooks | Edit Your Worksheets | Using Formulas and Functions | Working with Rows and Columns | Format Your Worksheets | Smart Formatting | Print Your Worksheets |

- Copy Formats
- **Create a Style**
- Apply a Style
- Change an Existing Style
- Format a Worksheet Automatically

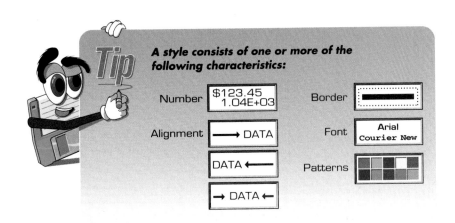

Tip

A style consists of one or more of the following characteristics:

Number	$123.45 1.04E+03	Border	
Alignment	→ DATA DATA ← → DATA ←	Font	Arial Courier New
		Patterns	

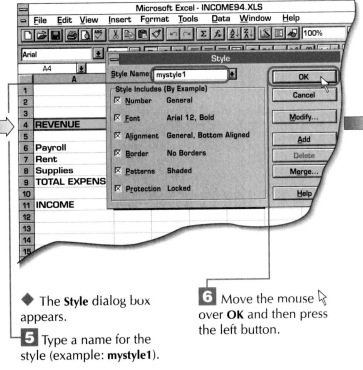

◆ The **Style** dialog box appears.

5 Type a name for the style (example: **mystyle1**).

6 Move the mouse over **OK** and then press the left button.

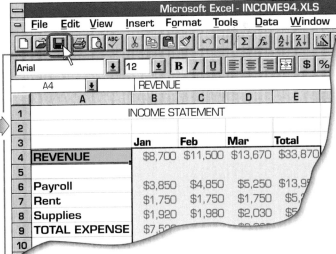

7 You must save your workbook to store the style. To do so, move the mouse over 🖫 and then press the left button.

Note: Once you create a style, you can apply it to any worksheet in the current workbook. To apply a style, refer to page 110.

APPLY A STYLE

After creating a style, you can apply it to cells in your worksheet. This keeps the appearance of cells consistent.

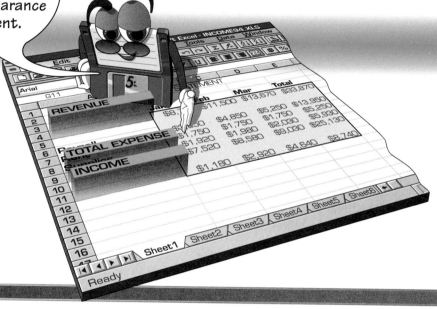

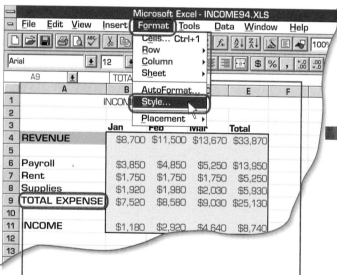

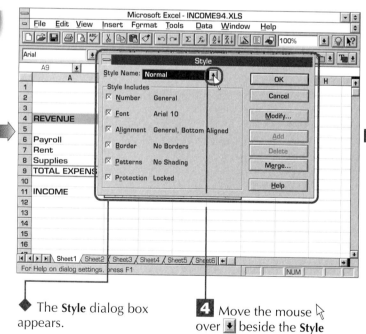

◆ The **Style** dialog box appears.

1 Select the cell(s) where you want to apply a style.

Note: To select cells, refer to page 12.

2 Move the mouse ⬡ over **Format** and then press the left button.

3 Move the mouse ⬡ over **Style** and then press the left button.

4 Move the mouse ⬡ over ⬇ beside the **Style Name:** box and then press the left button.

110

INTRODUCTION TO EXCEL

| Getting Started | Save and Open Your Workbooks | Edit Your Worksheets | Using Formulas and Functions | Working with Rows and Columns | Format Your Worksheets | Smart Formatting | Print Your Worksheets |

- Copy Formats
- Create a Style
- **Apply a Style**
- Change an Existing Style
- Format a Worksheet Automatically

Tip

You can change a style after you apply it to cells in your worksheet. This will change the appearance of all the cells assigned to the style at the same time. For more information on changing an existing style, refer to page 112.

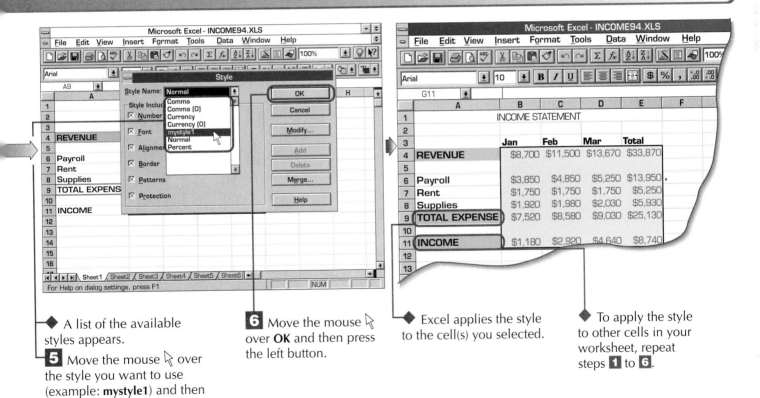

◆ A list of the available styles appears.

5 Move the mouse ⟨ over the style you want to use (example: **mystyle1**) and then press the left button.

6 Move the mouse ⟨ over **OK** and then press the left button.

◆ Excel applies the style to the cell(s) you selected.

◆ To apply the style to other cells in your worksheet, repeat steps **1** to **6**.

CHANGE AN EXISTING STYLE

You can easily change an existing style. All cells assigned to the original style will automatically display the new formats.

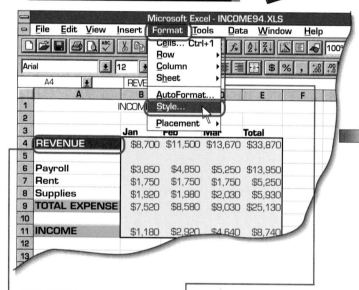

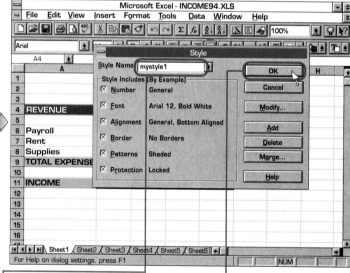

1 Make the desired formatting changes to a cell assigned to the style you want to change.

Note: To change the color of a cell in your worksheet, refer to page 102.

2 Select the cell.

3 Move the mouse ⟶ over **Format** and then press the left button.

4 Move the mouse ⟶ over **Style** and then press the left button.

◆ The **Style** dialog box appears.

◆ The **Style Name:** box displays the name of the style assigned to the cell you selected.

5 To change the style, retype the name (example: **mystyle1**).

6 Move the mouse ⟶ over **OK** and then press the left button.

112

INTRODUCTION TO EXCEL

| Getting Started | Save and Open Your Workbooks | Edit Your Worksheets | Using Formulas and Functions | Working with Rows and Columns | Format Your Worksheets | Smart Formatting | Print Your Worksheets |

- Copy Formats
- Create a Style
- Apply a Style
- **Change an Existing Style**
- Format a Worksheet Automatically

Styles are useful when you want all the headings in your worksheet to look the same. If you change the style of one of the headings, Excel will automatically change the appearance of all the others.

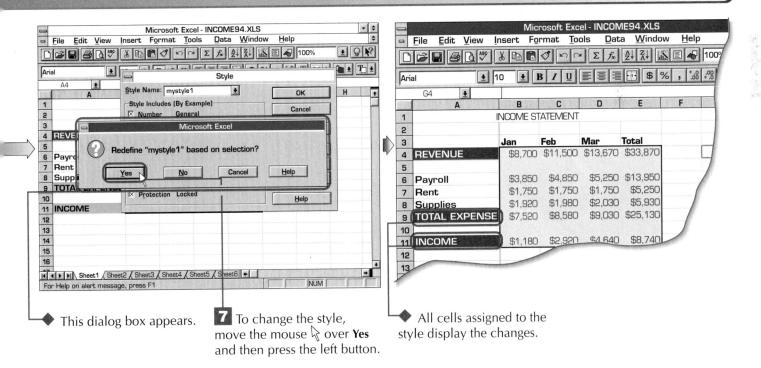

◆ This dialog box appears.

7 To change the style, move the mouse ⌖ over **Yes** and then press the left button.

◆ All cells assigned to the style display the changes.

FORMAT A WORKSHEET AUTOMATICALLY

Excel provides a selection of designs that you can choose from to quickly format your worksheet.

FORMAT A WORKSHEET AUTOMATICALLY

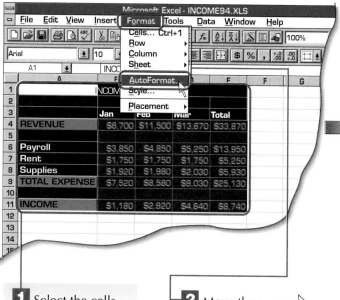

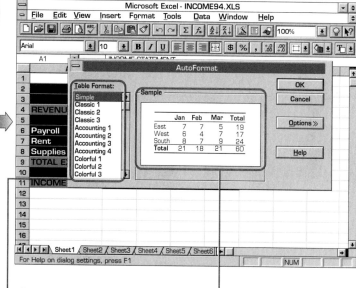

1 Select the cells you want to format.

Note: To select cells, refer to page 12.

2 Move the mouse over **Format** and then press the left button.

3 Move the mouse over **AutoFormat** and then press the left button.

◆ The **AutoFormat** dialog box appears.

◆ This area displays a list of the available designs.

◆ This area displays a sample of the highlighted design.

114

INTRODUCTION TO EXCEL

| Getting Started | Save and Open Your Workbooks | Edit Your Worksheets | Using Formulas and Functions | Working with Rows and Columns | Format Your Worksheets | Smart Formatting | Print Your Worksheets |

- Copy Formats
- Create a Style
- Apply a Style
- Change an Existing Style
- **Format a Worksheet Automatically**

To remove an AutoFormat design from your worksheet:

1 Select the cells displaying the design you want to remove.

Note: To select cells, refer to page 12.

2 Perform steps **2** to **5** below, selecting **None** in step **4**.

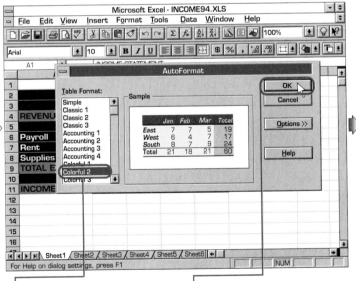

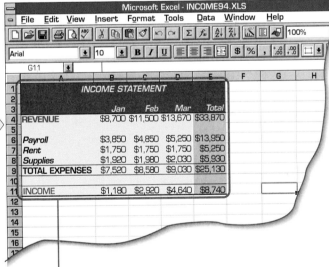

4 Press ↓ or ↑ on your keyboard until the **Sample** box displays the design you want to use (example: **Colorful 2**).

5 To select the highlighted design, move the mouse ↖ over **OK** and then press the left button.

◆ Excel applies the design to the cells you selected.

Note: To deselect cells, move the mouse ⊹ over any cell in your worksheet and then press the left button.

verview

PRINT YOUR WORKSHEETS

Preview a Worksheet

Change Margins

Print a Worksheet

Insert a Page Break

Change Print Options

Center Data on a Page

Change Page Orientation

Change Scaling

Print Titles

Add a Header or Footer

◆ In this chapter, you will learn how to print your worksheet and select from a variety of print options.

PREVIEW A WORKSHEET

The Print Preview feature lets you see on screen what your worksheet will look like when printed.

PREVIEW A WORKSHEET

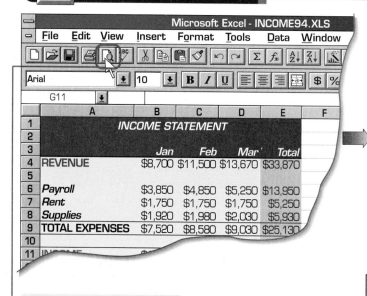

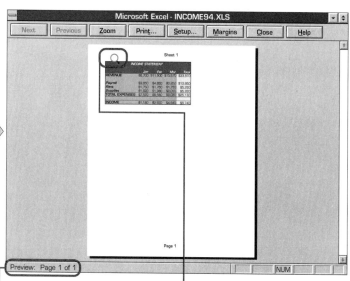

1 To display your worksheet in the Print Preview window, move the mouse ⬐ over 🔍 and then press the left button.

◆ The first page of your worksheet appears.

◆ The status bar at the bottom of your screen tells you which page you are viewing.

2 To magnify an area of the page, move the mouse ⬐ over the area (⬐ changes to 🔍) and then press the left button.

- **Preview a Worksheet**
- Change Margins
- Print a Worksheet
- Insert a Page Break
- Change Print Options
- Center Data on a Page
- Change Page Orientation
- Change Scaling
- Print Titles
- Add a Header or Footer

Tip

If your worksheet consists of more than one page, you can use these buttons to switch between the pages in the Print Preview window.

Next	Previous
◆ To view the next page, move the mouse over **Next** and then press the left button.	◆ To view the previous page, move the mouse over **Previous** and then press the left button.

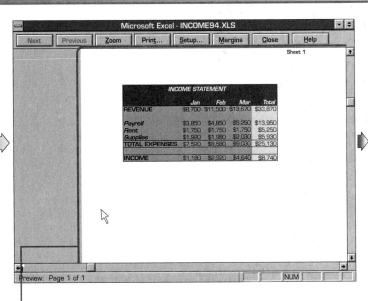

◆ A magnified view of the area appears.

◆ To browse through the page, press ⬇, ⬆, ➡ or ⬅ on your keyboard.

3 To again display the entire page, move the mouse anywhere over the page and then press the left button.

◆ The entire page appears on your screen.

4 To close the Print Preview window and return to your worksheet, move the mouse over **Close** and then press the left button.

CHANGE MARGINS

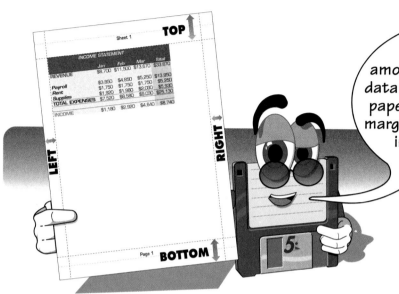

A margin is the amount of space between data and the edges of your paper. You can change the margins for your worksheet in the Print Preview window.

◆ When you begin a worksheet, the top and bottom margins are set at 1 inch. The left and right margins are set at 0.75 inches.

CHANGE MARGINS

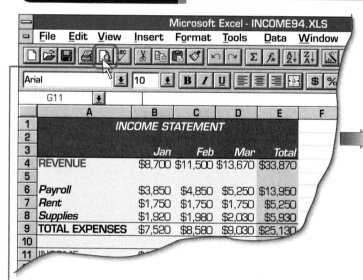

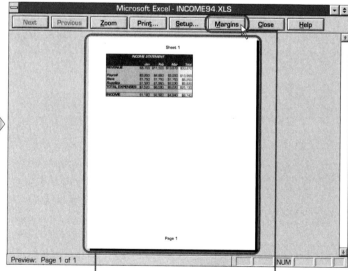

1 To display your worksheet in the Print Preview window, move the mouse ⍉ over 🔍 and then press the left button.

◆ The first page of your worksheet appears.

Note: For more information on using the Print Preview feature, refer to page 118.

2 To display the margins, move the mouse ⍉ over **Margins** and then press the left button.

Note: To hide the margins, repeat step 2.

Getting
Started

Save and
Open Your
Workbooks

Edit Your
Worksheets

Using
Formulas
and Functions

Working with
Rows and
Columns

Format Your
Worksheets

Smart
Formatting

* Preview a Worksheet
* **Change Margins**
* Print a Worksheet
* Insert a Page Break
* Change Print Options

* Center Data on a Page
* Change Page Orientation
* Change Scaling
* Print Titles
* Add a Header or Footer

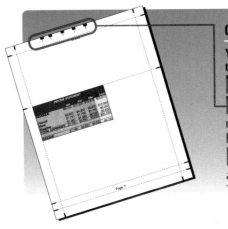

CHANGE COLUMN WIDTH

You can easily change the width of columns in the Print Preview window.

1 Perform steps **1** and **2** on page 120.

2 To change the width of a column, move the mouse ↳ over the column handle and ↳ changes to ↔.

3 Press and hold down the left button as you drag the column to a new width. Then release the button.

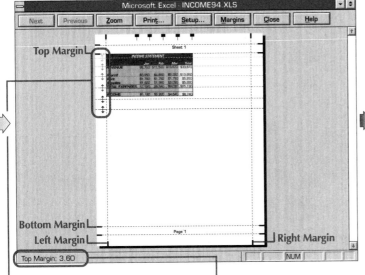

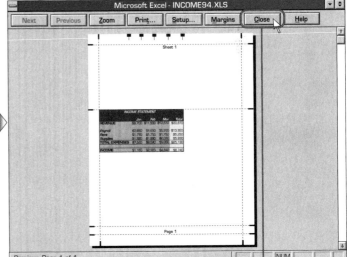

3 To change the position of a margin, move the mouse ↳ over the margin handle and ↳ changes to ↕ or ↔.

4 Press and hold down the left button as you drag the margin to a new location.

◆ A dotted line indicates the location of the new margin.

◆ The bottom of your screen displays the new measurement as you drag the margin.

5 Release the button to display the new margin.

6 To close the Print Preview window and return to your worksheet, move the mouse ↳ over **Close** and then press the left button.

Note: Margins are only visible when you display your worksheet in the Print Preview window.

121

PRINT A WORKSHEET

You can print a section of data or your entire worksheet. Before printing, make sure your printer is on and it contains paper.

PRINT A WORKSHEET

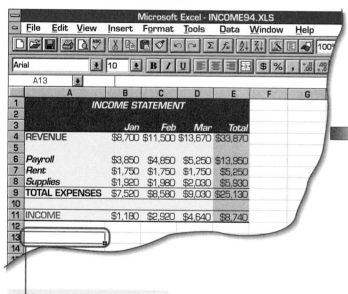

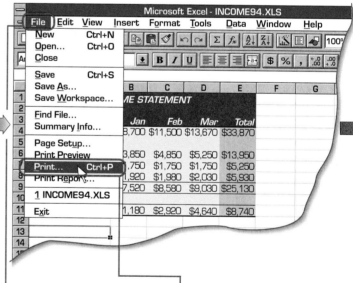

1 To print your entire worksheet, move the mouse over any cell in the worksheet and then press the left button.

◆ To print a section of your worksheet, select the cells you want to print.

Note: To select cells, refer to page 12.

2 Move the mouse over **File** and then press the left button.

3 Move the mouse over **Print** and then press the left button.

◆ The **Print** dialog box appears.

Getting Started	Save and Open Your Workbooks	Edit Your Worksheets	Using Formulas and Functions	Working with Rows and Columns	Format Your Worksheets	Smart Formatting	**Print Your Worksheets**

- Preview a Worksheet
- Change Margins
- **Print a Worksheet**
- Insert a Page Break
- Change Print Options

- Center Data on a Page
- Change Page Orientation
- Change Scaling
- Print Titles
- Add a Header or Footer

SHORTCUT

◆ To quickly print your entire worksheet, move the mouse ⇧ over 🖨 and then press the left button.

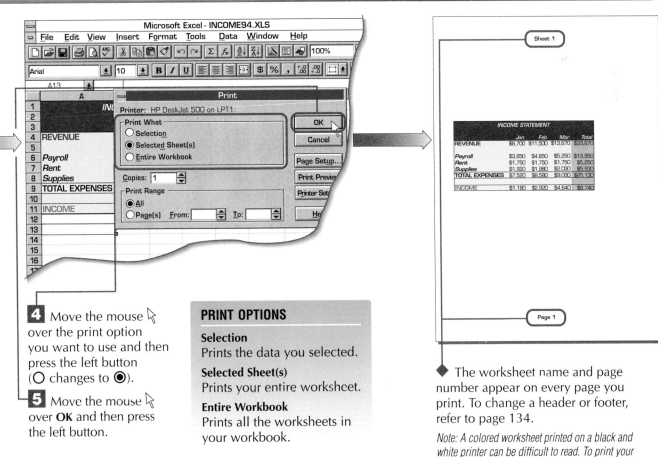

4 Move the mouse ⇧ over the print option you want to use and then press the left button (○ changes to ●).

5 Move the mouse ⇧ over **OK** and then press the left button.

PRINT OPTIONS

Selection
Prints the data you selected.

Selected Sheet(s)
Prints your entire worksheet.

Entire Workbook
Prints all the worksheets in your workbook.

◆ The worksheet name and page number appear on every page you print. To change a header or footer, refer to page 134.

Note: A colored worksheet printed on a black and white printer can be difficult to read. To print your worksheet in black and white, refer to page 126.

INSERT A PAGE BREAK

If you want to start a new page at a specific place in your worksheet, you can insert a page break. A page break defines where one page ends and another begins.

A page break you inserted.

If the data in your worksheet cannot fit on one page, Excel automatically starts a new one by inserting a page break.

A page break Excel inserted.

INSERT A HORIZONTAL PAGE BREAK

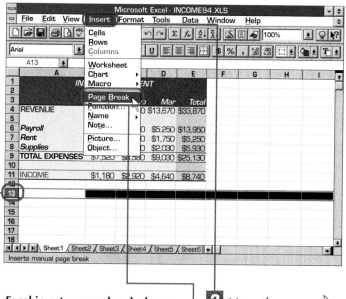

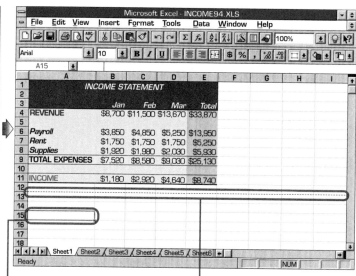

Excel inserts a page break above the row you select.

1 To select a row, move the mouse ⇩ over the row heading (example: **row 13**) and then press the left button.

2 Move the mouse ⇩ over **Insert** and then press the left button.

3 Move the mouse ⇩ over **Page Break** and then press the left button.

4 To view the page break, move the mouse ⇩ over any cell in your worksheet and then press the left button.

◆ A dashed line appears across your screen. This line defines where one page ends and another begins.

Note: This line will not appear when you print your worksheet.

Getting
Started

Save and
Open Your
Workbooks

Edit Your
Worksheets

Using
Formulas
and Functions

Working with
Rows and
Columns

Format Your
Worksheets

Smart
Formatting

**Print Your
Worksheets**

• Preview a Worksheet
• Change Margins
• Print a Worksheet
• **Insert a Page Break**
• Change Print Options

• Center Data on a Page
• Change Page Orientation
• Change Scaling
• Print Titles
• Add a Header or Footer

REMOVE A PAGE BREAK

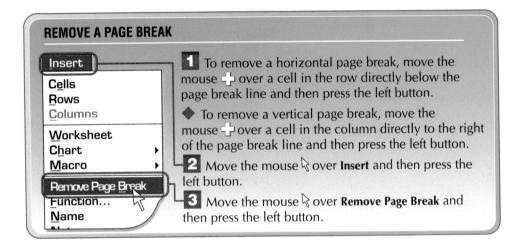

1 To remove a horizontal page break, move the mouse ✚ over a cell in the row directly below the page break line and then press the left button.

◆ To remove a vertical page break, move the mouse ✚ over a cell in the column directly to the right of the page break line and then press the left button.

2 Move the mouse ↘ over **Insert** and then press the left button.

3 Move the mouse ↘ over **Remove Page Break** and then press the left button.

INSERT A VERTICAL PAGE BREAK

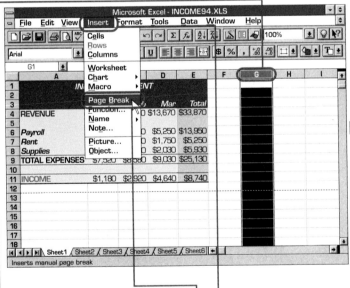

Excel inserts a page break to the left of the column you select.

1 To select a column, move the mouse ✚ over the column heading (example: **column G**) and then press the left button.

2 Move the mouse ↘ over **Insert** and then press the left button.

3 Move the mouse ↘ over **Page Break** and then press the left button.

4 To view the page break, move the mouse ✚ over any cell in your worksheet and then press the left button.

◆ A dashed line appears down your screen. This line defines where one page ends and another begins.

Note: This line will not appear when you print your worksheet.

125

CHANGE PRINT OPTIONS

You can use the Page Setup dialog box to change the way your worksheet appears on a printed page. The options you select will not change how the worksheet appears on your screen.

CHANGE PRINT OPTIONS

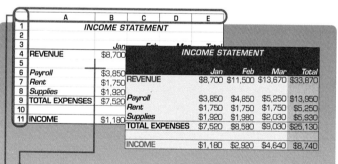

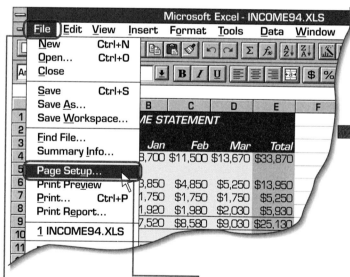

◆ **Gridlines** - prints lines that separate the cells in your worksheet.

◆ **Row and Column Headings** - prints the row and column headings as they appear on screen.

◆ **Black and White** - prints your worksheet in black and white. A colored worksheet printed on a black and white printer may be difficult to read. Use this option to avoid problems.

◆ **Draft Quality** - prints fewer graphics and does not print gridlines. This reduces printing time.

1 Move the mouse ↙ over **File** and then press the left button.

2 Move the mouse ↙ over **Page Setup** and then press the left button.

INTRODUCTION TO EXCEL

| Getting Started | Save and Open Your Workbooks | Edit Your Worksheets | Using Formulas and Functions | Working with Rows and Columns | Format Your Worksheets | Smart Formatting | **Print Your Worksheets** |

• Preview a Worksheet   • Center Data on a Page
• Change Margins   • Change Page Orientation
• Print a Worksheet   • Change Scaling
• Insert a Page Break   • Print Titles
• **Change Print Options** • Add a Header or Footer

The options you select in the **Page Setup** dialog box only affect the current worksheet.

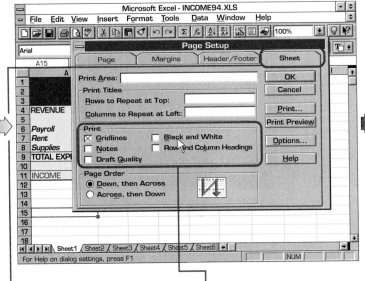

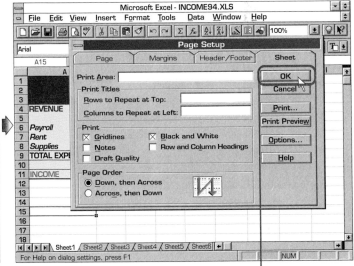

◆ The **Page Setup** dialog box appears.

3 Move the mouse ⬧ over the **Sheet** tab and then press the left button.

4 Move the mouse ⬧ over an option you want to use (example: **Black and White**) and then press the left button.

Note: ⊠ *indicates an option is on.*
☐ *indicates an option is off.*

5 Repeat step **4** for each option you want to use.

6 To confirm the change(s), move the mouse ⬧ over **OK** and then press the left button.

127

CENTER DATA ON A PAGE

CHANGE PAGE ORIENTATION

You can center data vertically and horizontally on a page.

CENTER DATA ON A PAGE

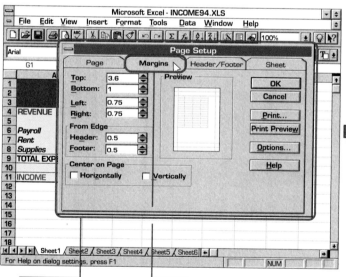

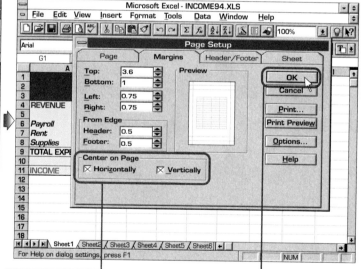

1 To center data on each page in your worksheet, display the **Page Setup** dialog box.

*Note: To display the **Page Setup** dialog box, perform steps **1** and **2** on page 126.*

2 Move the mouse ⌖ over the **Margins** tab and then press the left button.

3 To horizontally center data on a page, move the mouse ⌖ over **Horizontally** and then press the left button (☐ changes to ☒).

4 To vertically center data on a page, move the mouse ⌖ over **Vertically** and then press the left button (☐ changes to ☒).

◆ The **Preview** area displays what your page will look like when printed.

5 To confirm the changes, move the mouse ⌖ over **OK** and then press the left button.

Getting Started	Save and Open Your Workbooks	Edit Your Worksheets	Using Formulas and Functions	Working with Rows and Columns	Format Your Worksheets	Smart Formatting	**Print Your Worksheets**

- Preview a Worksheet
- Change Margins
- Print a Worksheet
- Insert a Page Break
- Change Print Options

- **Center Data on a Page**
- **Change Page Orientation**
- Change Scaling
- Print Titles
- Add a Header or Footer

If your worksheet is too wide to fit on one page, you can change its orientation.

Portrait
The worksheet prints across the short side of the paper. This is the initial (or default) setting.

Landscape
The worksheet prints across the long side of the paper.

CHANGE PAGE ORIENTATION

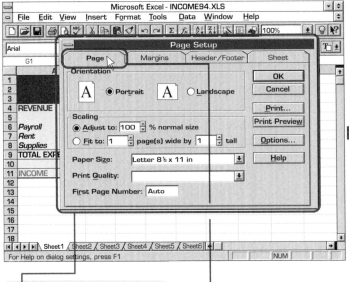

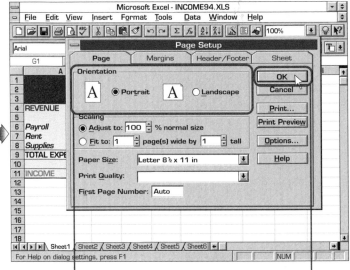

1 To change the orientation of each page in your worksheet, display the **Page Setup** dialog box.

*Note: To display the **Page Setup** dialog box, perform steps **1** and **2** on page 126.*

2 Move the mouse ⬚ over the **Page** tab and then press the left button.

3 Move the mouse ⬚ over the orientation you want to use and then press the left button (○ changes to ●).

4 To confirm the change, move the mouse ⬚ over **OK** and then press the left button.

129

CHANGE SCALING

You can use the scaling feature to increase or decrease the size of data on a printed page. This is helpful when you want to fit your data on a specific number of pages.

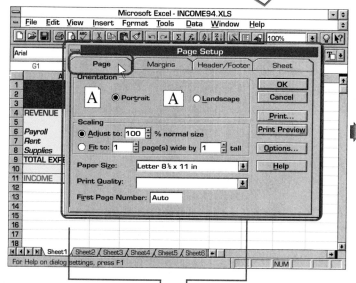

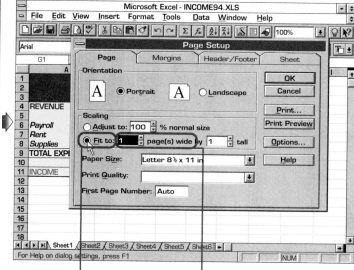

When you change the scaling of your worksheet, the changes only affect the printout. The data on your screen does not change.

1 Display the **Page Setup** dialog box.

*Note: To display the **Page Setup** dialog box, perform steps **1** and **2** on page 126.*

2 Move the mouse ⌖ over the **Page** tab and then press the left button.

3 Move the mouse ⌖ over **Fit to**: and then press the left button (○ changes to ◉).

4 Type the number of pages you want your data to extend across (example: **1**).

130

Getting Started	Save and Open Your Workbooks	Edit Your Worksheets	Using Formulas and Functions	Working with Rows and Columns	Format Your Worksheets	Smart Formatting	**Print Your Worksheets**

- Preview a Worksheet
- Change Margins
- Print a Worksheet
- Insert a Page Break
- Change Print Options

- Center Data on a Page
- Change Page Orientation
- **Change Scaling**
- Print Titles
- Add a Header or Footer

Tip

To fit data on a specific number of pages, you must specify the number of pages you want your data to extend down and across.

This feature is useful if the last page of your worksheet contains a small amount of data. You can change the scaling to fit the data on one less page.

Across
(3 Pages Wide)

Down
(2 Pages Tall)

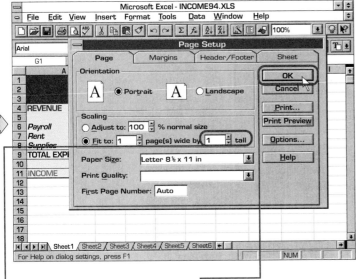

You can manually change the size of data on the printout using the Page Setup dialog box. The size of data on your screen will not change.

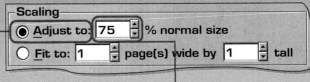

Scaling
- (●) **Adjust to:** `75` % normal size
- ( ) **Fit to:** `1` page(s) wide by `1` tall

1 Perform steps **1** and **2** on page 130.

2 Move the mouse over **Adjust to:** and then press the left button (○ changes to ●).

3 Type the percentage you want to use.

Note: If the percentage you type is less than 100, Excel will decrease the print size. If the percentage you type is greater than 100, Excel will increase the print size.

4 To confirm the change, move the mouse over **OK** and then press the left button.

5 Press **Tab** on your keyboard.

6 Type the number of pages you want your data to extend down (example: **1**).

7 To confirm the changes, move the mouse over **OK** and then press the left button.

You can use data from your worksheet as titles on each printed page. Titles make your data easier to understand.

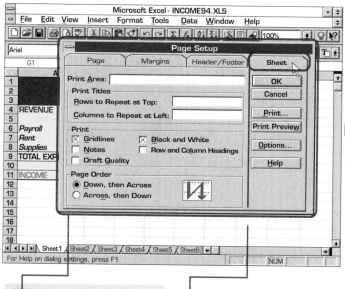

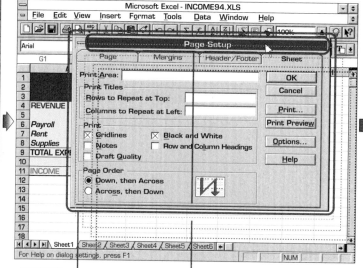

1 To print titles on each printed page of your worksheet, display the **Page Setup** dialog box.

*Note: To display the **Page Setup** dialog box, perform steps* **1** *and* **2** *on page 126.*

2 Move the mouse over the **Sheet** tab and then press the left button.

◆ You can move the **Page Setup** dialog box if it covers the rows or columns you want to use as titles.

3 To move the dialog box, move the mouse over the title bar.

4 Press and hold down the left button as you drag the dialog box to a new location on your screen. Then release the button.

Getting Started	Save and Open Your Workbooks	Edit Your Worksheets	Using Formulas and Functions	Working with Rows and Columns	Format Your Worksheets	Smart Formatting	**Print Your Worksheets**

- Preview a Worksheet
- Change Margins
- Print a Worksheet
- Insert a Page Break
- Change Print Options

- Center Data on a Page
- Change Page Orientation
- Change Scaling
- **Print Titles**
- Add a Header or Footer

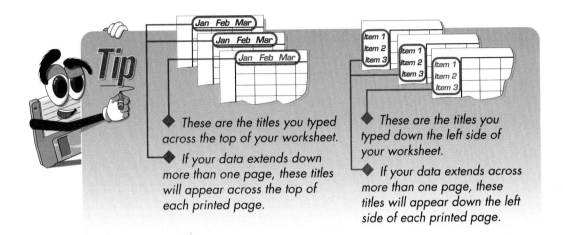

♦ These are the titles you typed across the top of your worksheet.

♦ If your data extends down more than one page, these titles will appear across the top of each printed page.

♦ These are the titles you typed down the left side of your worksheet.

♦ If your data extends across more than one page, these titles will appear down the left side of each printed page.

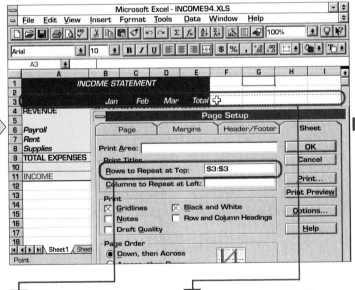

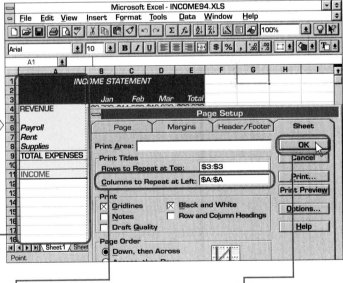

5 To print titles across the top of each printed page, move the mouse I over the box beside **Rows to Repeat at Top:** and then press the left button.

6 Move the mouse ⊹ over a cell in the row containing the titles you want to print (example: **row 3**) and then press the left button.

7 To print titles down the left side of each printed page, move the mouse I over the box beside **Columns to Repeat at Left:** and then press the left button.

8 Move the mouse ⊹ over a cell in the column containing the titles you want to print (example: **column A**) and then press the left button.

9 To confirm the changes, move the mouse ⟡ over **OK** and then press the left button.

ADD A HEADER OR FOOTER

Headers and footers print information at the top and bottom of each page.

Sheet 1

Header

Excel automatically prints the name of the worksheet at the top of each page. You can change this header at any time.

Footer

Excel automatically prints the page number at the bottom of each page. You can change this footer at any time.

Page 1

ADD A HEADER OR FOOTER

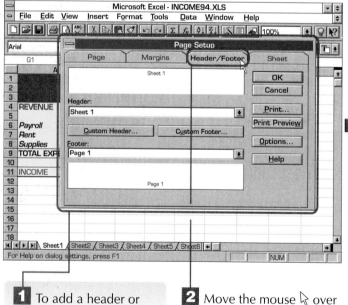

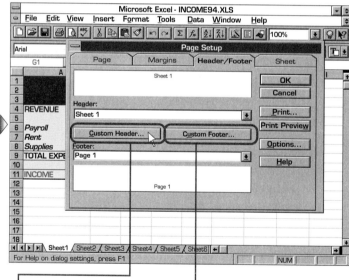

1 To add a header or footer, display the **Page Setup** dialog box.

*Note: To display the **Page Setup** dialog box, perform steps **1** and **2** on page 126.*

2 Move the mouse ⟍ over the **Header/Footer** tab and then press the left button.

3 To create a header, move the mouse ⟍ over **Custom Header** and then press the left button.

◆ To create a footer, move the mouse ⟍ over **Custom Footer** and then press the left button.

134

| Getting Started | Save and Open Your Workbooks | Edit Your Worksheets | Using Formulas and Functions | Working with Rows and Columns | Format Your Worksheets | Smart Formatting | **Print Your Worksheets** |

- Preview a Worksheet
- Change Margins
- Print a Worksheet
- Insert a Page Break
- Change Print Options

- Center Data on a Page
- Change Page Orientation
- Change Scaling
- Print Titles
- **Add a Header or Footer**

In the Header or Footer dialog box you can use these buttons to change the appearance of a header or footer or add additional information.

 Inserts the page number.

 Inserts the current time.

 Inserts the total number of pages in your worksheet.

 Inserts the name of the workbook.

 *Displays the **Font** dialog box so you can format text you have selected.*

Inserts the current date.

 Inserts the name of the worksheet.

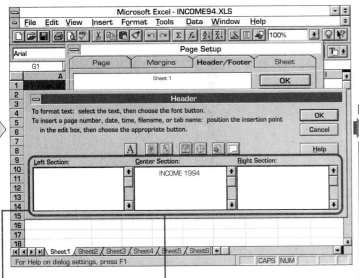

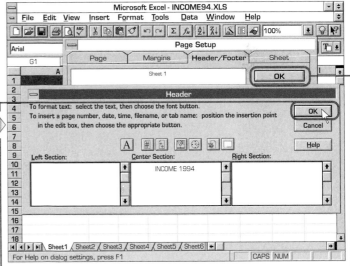

4 Move the mouse ⌖ over the box under **Center Section:** and then press the left button.

5 To remove the existing text, press `Delete` or `◆Backspace` on your keyboard until the text disappears.

6 Move the mouse ⌖ over the box for the area of the page where you want to display the header or footer (example: **Center Section:**) and then press the left button.

7 Type the text (example: **INCOME 1994**).

8 Move the mouse ⌖ over **OK** and then press the left button.

9 Move the mouse ⌖ over **OK** in the **Page Setup** dialog box and then press the left button.

*Note: Headers and footers are only visible when you display your worksheet in the **Print Preview** window. For more information, refer to page 118.*

135

verview

CHANGE YOUR SCREEN DISPLAY

Zoom In or Out

Display or Hide Toolbars

Freeze Rows and Columns

Split the Screen

◆ In this chapter, you will learn to change the way your worksheet appears on screen.

ZOOM IN OR OUT

You can magnify a worksheet to read small data or shrink a worksheet to view more of your data.

ZOOM TO A SPECIFIC PERCENTAGE

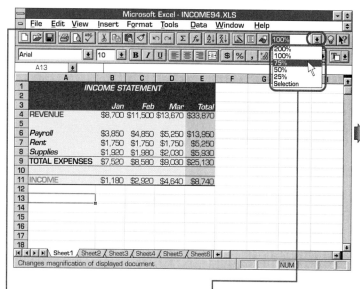

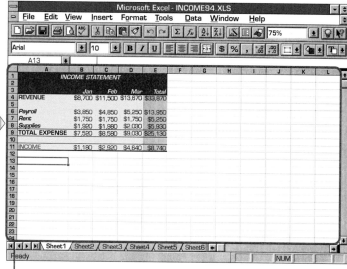

When you first start Excel, your worksheet appears in the 100% zoom setting.

1 To display your worksheet using a different setting, move the mouse ⍓ over ⬇ beside the **Zoom Control** box and then press the left button.

◆ A list of zoom settings appears.

2 Move the mouse ⍓ over the zoom setting you want to use (example: **75%**) and then press the left button.

◆ Your worksheet appears in the new zoom setting.

Note: When you change the zoom setting, the changes will not affect the way the data appears on a printed page.

138

| Change Your Screen Display | Using Multiple Worksheets | Using Multiple Workbooks | Charting Data | Enhance a Chart | Drawing Objects | Manage Data in a List |

- **Zoom In or Out**
- Display or Hide Toolbars
- Freeze Rows and Columns
- Split the Screen

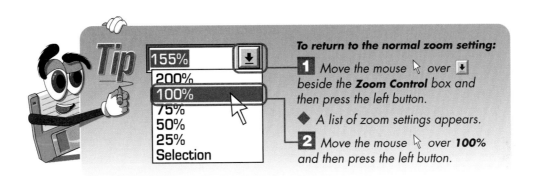

To return to the normal zoom setting:

1 Move the mouse ⟍ over ⬇ beside the **Zoom Control** box and then press the left button.

◆ A list of zoom settings appears.

2 Move the mouse ⟍ over **100%** and then press the left button.

ZOOM DATA TO FILL THE SCREEN

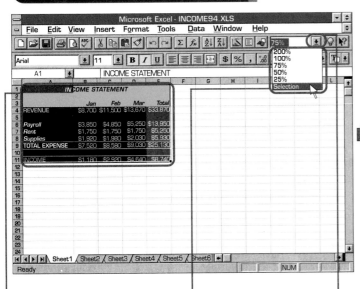

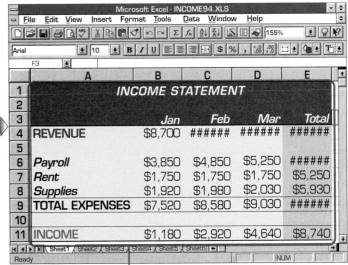

You can enlarge or reduce a section of data to fill your screen.

1 Select the cells containing the data you want to fill the screen.

Note: To select cells, refer to page 12.

2 Move the mouse ⟍ over ⬇ beside the **Zoom Control** box and then press the left button.

◆ A list of zoom settings appears.

3 Move the mouse ⟍ over **Selection** and then press the left button.

◆ The data in the cells you selected fills the screen.

Note: To deselect cells, move the mouse ⌖ over any cell in your worksheet and then press the left button.

Note: If number signs (#) appear in a cell, the column is not wide enough to display the entire number. To change the column width, refer to page 82.

139

DISPLAY OR HIDE TOOLBARS

Excel offers thirteen different toolbars that you can display or hide at any time. Each toolbar contains a series of buttons that let you quickly select commands.

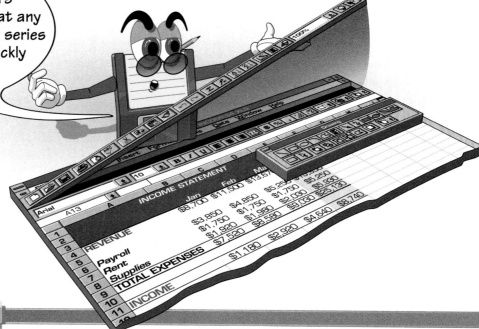

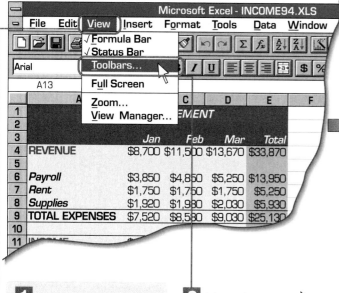

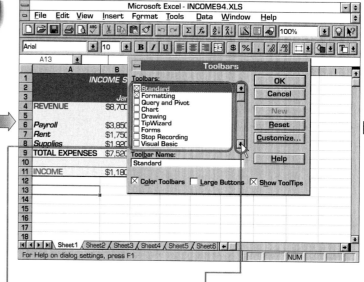

1 To display or hide a toolbar, move the mouse over **View** and then press the left button.

2 Move the mouse over **Toolbars** and then press the left button.

◆ The **Toolbars** dialog box appears.

◆ This area displays a list of the available toolbars.

3 To view more toolbar names, move the mouse over ▼ or ▲ and then press the left button.

140

| Change Your Screen Display | Using Multiple Worksheets | Using Multiple Workbooks | Charting Data | Enhance a Chart | Drawing Objects | Manage Data in a List |

- Zoom In or Out
- **Display or Hide Toolbars**
- Freeze Rows and Columns
- Split the Screen

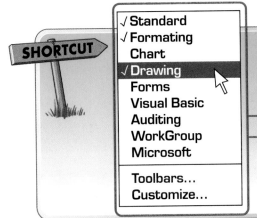

SHORTCUT

✓ **Standard**
✓ **Formating**
Chart
✓ **Drawing**
Forms
Visual Basic
Auditing
WorkGroup
Microsoft

Toolbars...
Customize...

To quickly display or hide a toolbar:

1 Move the mouse ⌖ anywhere over a toolbar on your screen and then press the **right** mouse button.

◆ A list of toolbars appears.

2 Move the mouse ⌖ over the toolbar you want to display or hide and then press the left button.

Note: ✓ beside a toolbar name indicates the toolbar is currently displayed on your screen.

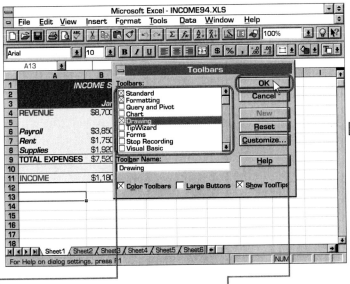

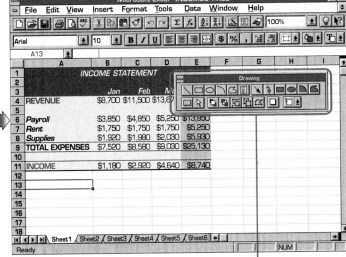

4 To display a toolbar, move the mouse ⌖ over the toolbar name and then press the left button (☐ changes to ☒).

◆ To hide a toolbar, move the mouse ⌖ over the toolbar name and then press the left button (☒ changes to ☐).

5 Move the mouse ⌖ over **OK** and then press the left button.

◆ Excel displays or hides the toolbar(s) you selected.

Note: A screen displaying fewer toolbars provides a larger and less cluttered working area.

141

FREEZE ROWS AND COLUMNS

You can freeze rows and columns in your worksheet so they will not move. This is useful for moving through data in a large worksheet while keeping your headings on the screen.

FREEZE ROWS AND COLUMNS

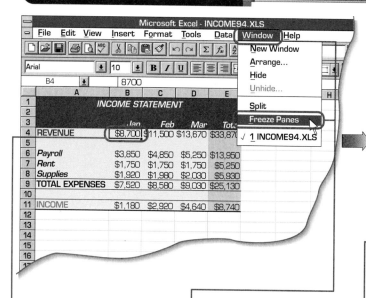

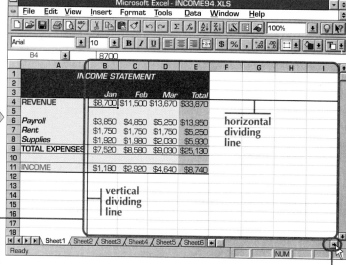

Excel will freeze the cells above and to the left of the cell you select.

1 To select a cell, move the mouse ⌗ over the cell (example: **B4**) and then press the left button.

2 Move the mouse ⇗ over **Window** and then press the left button.

3 Move the mouse ⇗ over **Freeze Panes** and then press the left button.

◆ Vertical and horizontal dividing lines appear on your screen.

◆ You can shift the columns on the right side of the vertical dividing line. The column(s) to the left of the line will not move.

4 To shift the columns to the left, move the mouse ⇗ over ➡ and then press the left button.

Change Your Screen Display	Using Multiple Worksheets	Using Multiple Workbooks	Charting Data	Enhance a Chart	Drawing Objects	Manage Data in a List

- Zoom In or Out
- Display or Hide Toolbars
- **Freeze Rows and Columns**
- Split the Screen

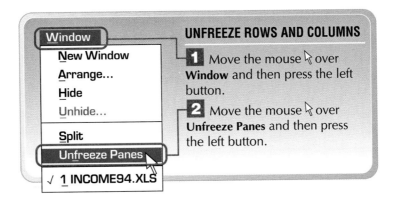

Window

New Window

Arrange...

Hide

Unhide...

Split

Unfreeze Panes

✓ 1 INCOME94.XLS

UNFREEZE ROWS AND COLUMNS

1 Move the mouse over **Window** and then press the left button.

2 Move the mouse over **Unfreeze Panes** and then press the left button.

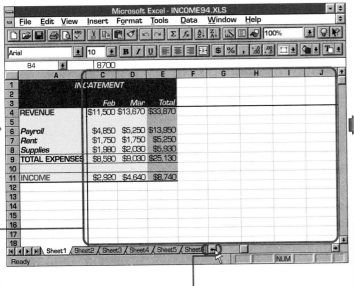

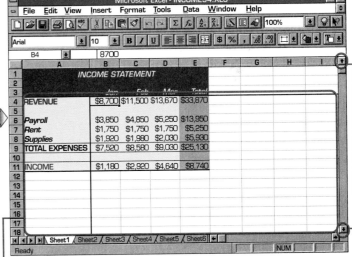

◆ The columns on the right side of the dividing line shift left one column.

*Note: In this example, column **B** is hidden behind the dividing line.*

5 To shift the columns to the right, move the mouse over ◄ and then press the left button.

◆ You can shift the rows below the horizontal dividing line. The row(s) above the line will not move.

◆ To shift the rows upward, move the mouse over ▼ and then press the left button.

◆ To shift the rows downward, move the mouse over ▲ and then press the left button.

You can split your screen into four separate sections. This lets you view different areas of a large worksheet at the same time.

SPLIT THE SCREEN

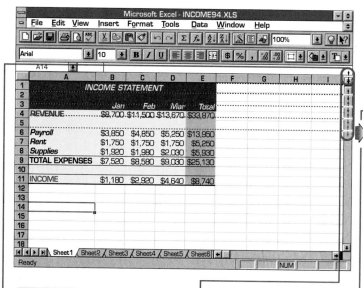

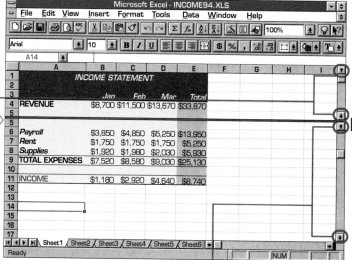

1 To split your screen horizontally in two sections, move the mouse over this split box (changes to ↨).

2 Press and hold down the left button as you drag the box where you want to split the screen.

3 Release the button and the screen splits horizontally in two.

◆ To move through the rows above the dividing line, move the mouse over ↑ or ↓ and then press the left button.

◆ To move through the rows below the dividing line, move the mouse over ↑ or ↓ and then press the left button.

Change Your Screen Display	Using Multiple Worksheets	Using Multiple Workbooks	Charting Data	Enhance a Chart	Drawing Objects	Manage Data in a List

- Zoom In or Out
- Display or Hide Toolbars
- Freeze Rows and Columns
- **Split the Screen**

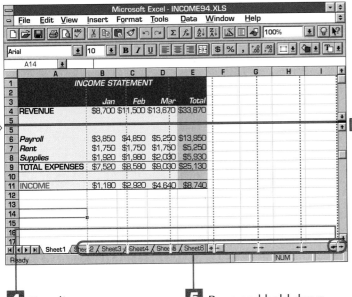

Window

New Window

Arrange...

Hide

Unhide...

Remove Split

Freeze Panes

√ 1 INCOME94.XLS

REMOVE SPLIT

1 To remove the dividing lines from your screen, move the mouse ⃗ over **Window** and then press the left button.

2 Move the mouse ⃗ over **Remove Split** and then press the left button.

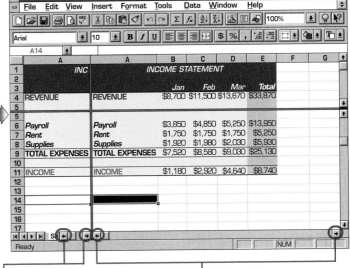

4 To split your screen vertically in two sections, move the mouse ⃗ over this split box (⃗ changes to ↔).

5 Press and hold down the left button as you drag the box where you want to split the screen.

6 Release the button and the screen splits vertically in two.

◆ To move through the columns to the left of the dividing line, move the mouse ⃗ over ◄ or ► and then press the left button.

◆ To move through the columns to the right of the dividing line, move the mouse ⃗ over ◄ or ► and then press the left button.

USING MULTIPLE WORKSHEETS

Switch Between Worksheets

Name a Worksheet

Copy or Move Data Between Worksheets

Link Data Across Worksheets

Enter a Formula Across Worksheets

Delete a Worksheet

◆ In this chapter, you will learn how to work with more than one worksheet in a workbook.

SWITCH BETWEEN WORKSHEETS

The worksheet displayed on your screen is part of a workbook. Like a three-ring binder, a workbook contains several sheets that you can easily flip through. This lets you view the contents of each worksheet.

SWITCH BETWEEN WORKSHEETS

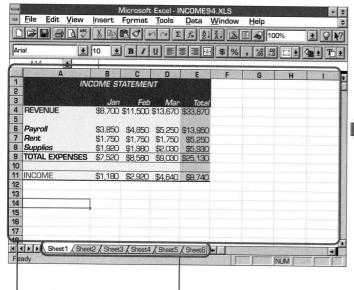

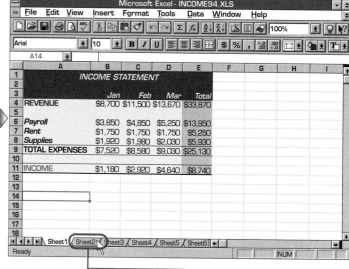

◆ The worksheet displayed on your screen is one of 16 worksheets in the current workbook.

◆ The current worksheet displays a white tab.

◆ The other worksheets display gray tabs.

◆ The contents of the current worksheet are displayed on your screen. The contents of the other worksheets are hidden behind this worksheet.

1 To display the contents of another worksheet, move the mouse ⌖ over the worksheet tab (example: **Sheet2**) and then press the left button.

Change Your Screen Display	Using Multiple Worksheets	Using Multiple Workbooks	Charting Data	Enhance a Chart	Drawing Objects	Manage Data in a List

- **Switch Between Worksheets**
- Name a Worksheet
- Copy or Move Data Between Worksheets
- Link Data Across Worksheets
- Enter a Formula Across Worksheets
- Delete a Worksheet

Tip

You can use the worksheets in a workbook to store related information. For example, you can store information for each division of a company on separate worksheets.

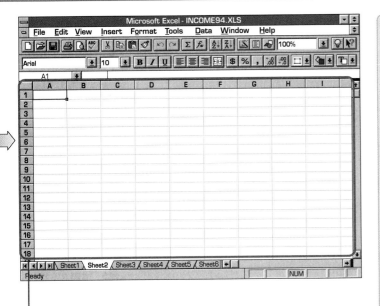

◆ The contents of the worksheet appear.

Excel cannot fit the names of all the worksheets at the bottom of your screen. You can use these arrows to display the other worksheet tabs.

To display the first worksheet tab, move the mouse over ◄ and then press the left button.

To scroll left through the worksheet tabs, move the mouse over ◄ and then press the left button.

To scroll right through the worksheet tabs, move the mouse over ► and then press the left button.

To display the last worksheet tab, move the mouse over ►I and then press the left button.

149

NAME A WORKSHEET

You can give each worksheet in a workbook a descriptive name. This helps you remember where you stored your data.

NAME A WORKSHEET

RULES FOR NAMING A WORKSHEET

A worksheet name can contain up to 31 characters, including:

◆ The letters A to Z, upper or lower case

◆ The numbers 0 to 9

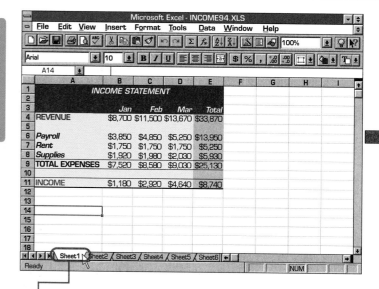

1 To change the name of a worksheet, move the mouse over the worksheet tab and then quickly press the left button twice.

| Change Your Screen Display | Using Multiple Worksheets | Using Multiple Workbooks | Charting Data | Enhance a Chart | Drawing Objects | Manage Data in a List |

- Switch Between Worksheets
- **Name a Worksheet**
- Copy or Move Data Between Worksheets
- Link Data Across Worksheets
- Enter a Formula Across Worksheets
- Delete a Worksheet

Tip

Excel names the worksheets Sheet1 through Sheet16. You can name one or all of these worksheets.

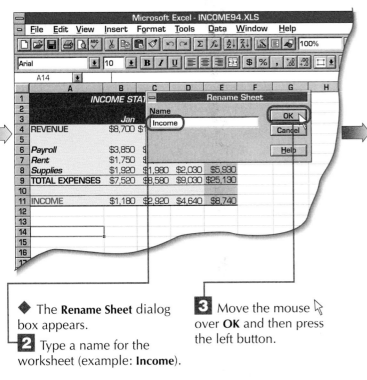

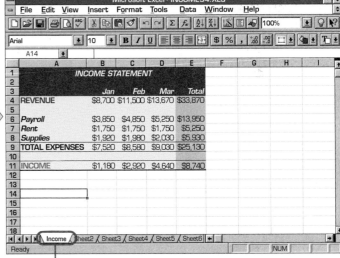

◆ The **Rename Sheet** dialog box appears.

2 Type a name for the worksheet (example: **Income**).

3 Move the mouse over **OK** and then press the left button.

◆ The worksheet tab displays the new name.

COPY OR MOVE DATA BETWEEN WORKSHEETS

Copying or moving data between worksheets saves you time when you are working in one worksheet and want to use data from another.

COPY OR MOVE DATA BETWEEN WORKSHEETS

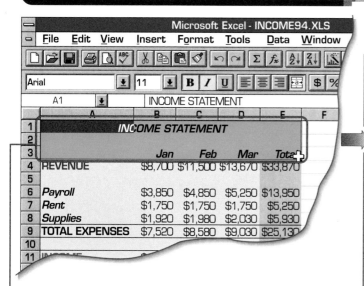

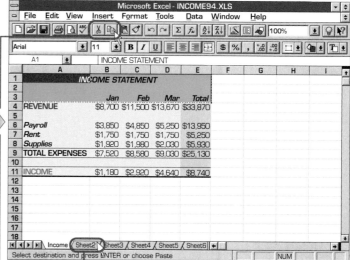

1 Select the cells containing the data you want to copy or move to another worksheet.

Note: To select cells, refer to page 12.

2 To copy the data, move the mouse ⟍ over 📋 and then press the left button.

◆ To move the data, move the mouse ⟍ over ✂ and then press the left button.

3 Move the mouse ⟍ over the tab of the worksheet where you want to place the data and then press the left button.

- Switch Between Worksheets
- Name a Worksheet
- **Copy or Move Data Between Worksheets**
- Link Data Across Worksheets
- Enter a Formula Across Worksheets
- Delete a Worksheet

COPY DATA

When you copy data, Excel copies the data and pastes the copy in a new location. The original data remains in its place.

MOVE DATA

When you move data, Excel cuts the data and pastes it in a new location. The original data disappears.

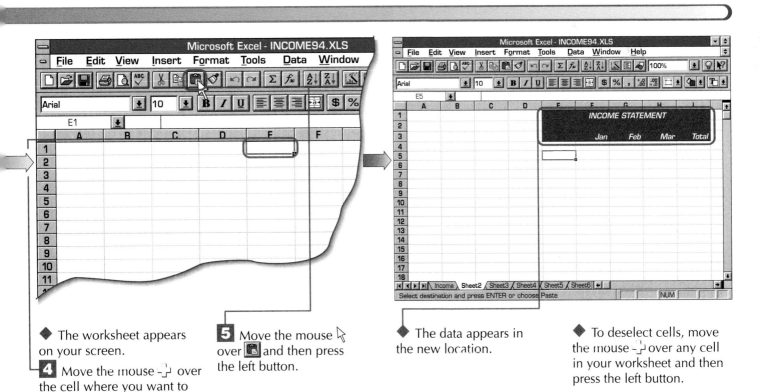

◆ The worksheet appears on your screen.

4 Move the mouse ⌖ over the cell where you want to place the data and then press the left button. This cell will become the top left cell of the new location.

5 Move the mouse ⌖ over 📋 and then press the left button.

◆ The data appears in the new location.

◆ To deselect cells, move the mouse ⌖ over any cell in your worksheet and then press the left button.

LINK DATA ACROSS WORKSHEETS

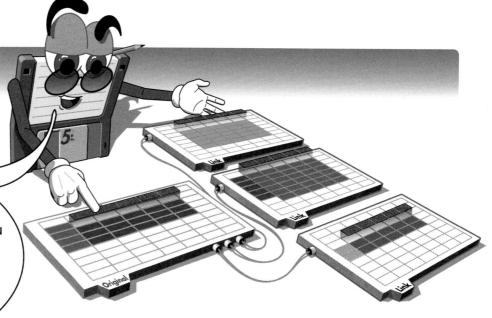

If you want a worksheet to always display the same data as another, you can link the data. This way, if you change the data in the original worksheet, the data in the linked worksheet will also change.

LINK DATA ACROSS WORKSHEETS

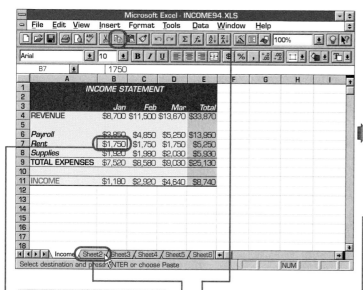

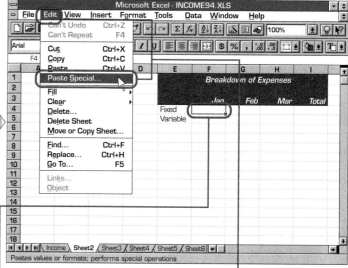

1 Move the mouse ⊹ over a cell containing data you want to link to another worksheet and then press the left button.

2 To copy the data, move the mouse ⇖ over 📋 and then press the left button.

3 Move the mouse ⇖ over the tab of the worksheet where you want to link the data and then press the left button.

◆ The worksheet appears on your screen.

4 Move the mouse ⊹ over the cell where you want to place the data and then press the left button.

5 Move the mouse ⇖ over **Edit** and then press the left button.

6 Move the mouse ⇖ over **Paste Special** and then press the left button.

154

Change Your Screen Display	Using Multiple Worksheets	Using Multiple Workbooks	Charting Data	Enhance a Chart	Drawing Objects	Manage Data in a List

- Switch Between Worksheets
- Name a Worksheet
- Copy or Move Data Between Worksheets
- **Link Data Across Worksheets**
- Enter a Formula Across Worksheets
- Delete a Worksheet

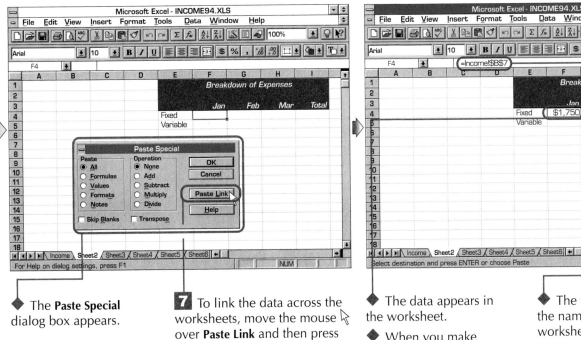

♦ The **Paste Special** dialog box appears.

7 To link the data across the worksheets, move the mouse over **Paste Link** and then press the left button.

♦ The data appears in the worksheet.

♦ When you make changes to the data in the original worksheet, the linked worksheet will automatically display the changes.

♦ The formula bar displays the name of the original worksheet and the linked cell.

155

ENTER A FORMULA ACROSS WORKSHEETS

You can enter a formula in one worksheet that uses data from other worksheets.

ENTER A FORMULA ACROSS WORKSHEETS

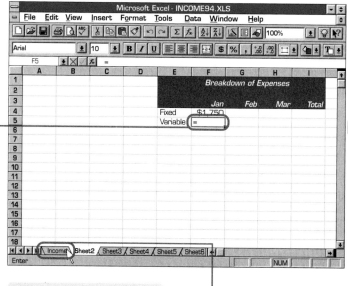

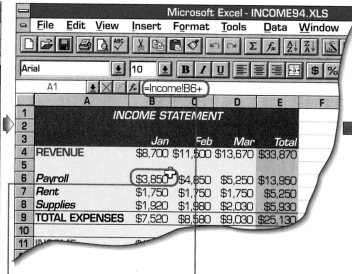

1 Move the mouse ⊕ over the cell where you want to display the result of the formula and then press the left button.

2 To begin the formula, type an equal sign (**=**).

3 Move the mouse ⌖ over the tab of the worksheet containing the data you want to use in the formula and then press the left button.

◆ The worksheet appears on your screen.

4 Move the mouse ⊕ over a cell containing the data you want to use in the formula (example: **B6**) and then press the left button.

5 Type an operator for the formula (example: **+**).

Change Your Screen Display	Using Multiple Worksheets	Using Multiple Workbooks	Charting Data	Enhance a Chart	Drawing Objects	Manage Data in a List

- Switch Between Worksheets
- Name a Worksheet
- Copy or Move Data Between Worksheets
- Link Data Across Worksheets
- **Enter a Formula Across Worksheets**
- Delete a Worksheet

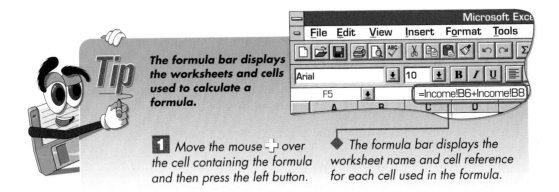

Tip

The formula bar displays the worksheets and cells used to calculate a formula.

1 Move the mouse ⊕ over the cell containing the formula and then press the left button.

◆ The formula bar displays the worksheet name and cell reference for each cell used in the formula.

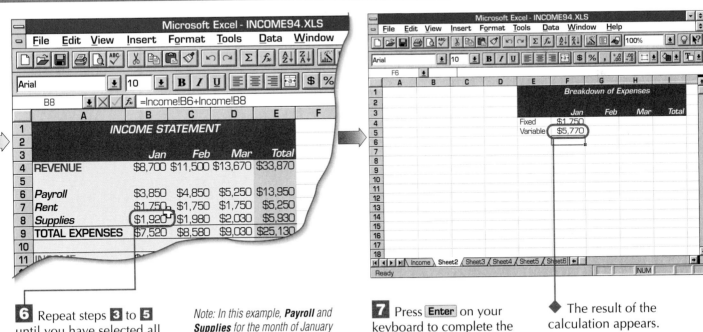

6 Repeat steps **3** to **5** until you have selected all the cells containing the data you want to use in the formula.

*Note: In this example, **Payroll** and **Supplies** for the month of January are added together.*

7 Press **Enter** on your keyboard to complete the formula.

◆ The result of the calculation appears.

DELETE A WORKSHEET

You can permanently remove a worksheet from a workbook that you no longer need.

DELETE A WORKSHEET

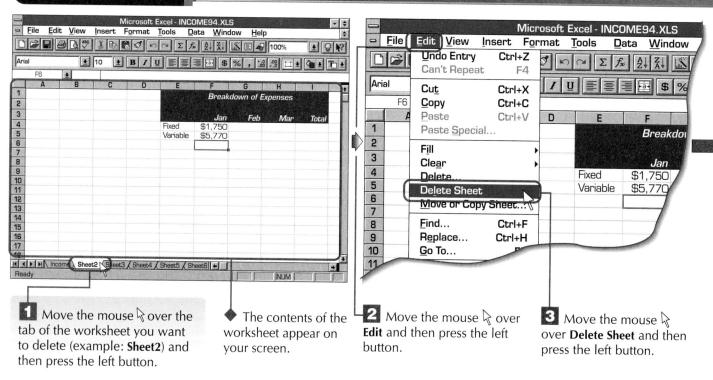

1 Move the mouse ⌖ over the tab of the worksheet you want to delete (example: **Sheet2**) and then press the left button.

◆ The contents of the worksheet appear on your screen.

2 Move the mouse ⌖ over **Edit** and then press the left button.

3 Move the mouse ⌖ over **Delete Sheet** and then press the left button.

| Change Your Screen Display | Using Multiple Worksheets | Using Multiple Workbooks | Charting Data | Enhance a Chart | Drawing Objects | Manage Data in a List |

- Switch Between Worksheets
- Name a Worksheet
- Copy or Move Data Between Worksheets
- Link Data Across Worksheets
- Enter a Formula Across Worksheets
- **Delete a Worksheet**

IMPORTANT!

Do not delete a worksheet you may need in the future. Once you delete a worksheet, Excel erases the data from your computer's memory.

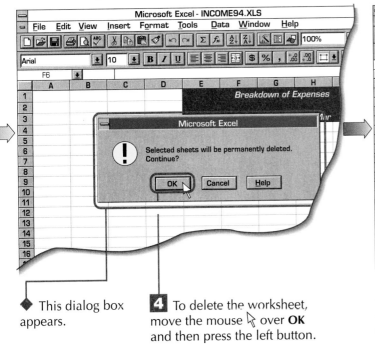

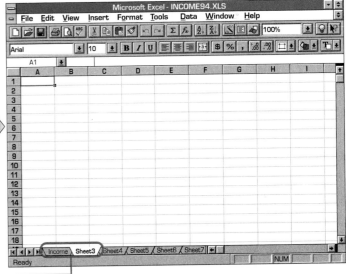

◆ This dialog box appears.

4 To delete the worksheet, move the mouse � over **OK** and then press the left button.

◆ Excel removes the worksheet from your workbook.

◆ The next worksheet in your workbook appears on the screen.

Overview

USING MULTIPLE WORKBOOKS

Create a New Workbook

Switch Between Workbooks

Arrange Open Workbooks

Close a Workbook

Maximize a Workbook

◆ In this chapter, you will learn how to create a new workbook and display more than one workbook at a time.

You can create a new workbook to store data on a different topic. Excel lets you easily switch between all of your open workbooks.

CREATE A NEW WORKBOOK

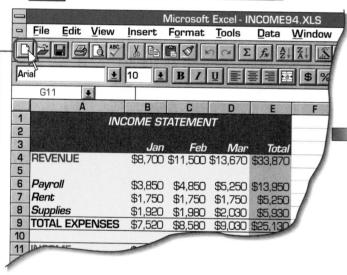

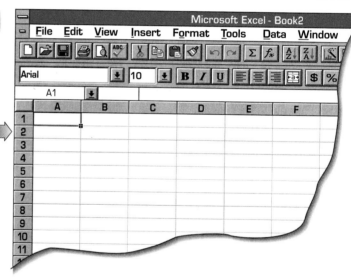

1 To create a new workbook, move the mouse ⟍ over 🗋 and then press the left button.

◆ A new workbook appears.

Note: The previous workbook is now hidden behind the new workbook.

Tip

Think of each new workbook as a new 3-ring binder. Each workbook contains worksheets that you can use to organize your data.

SWITCH BETWEEN WORKBOOKS

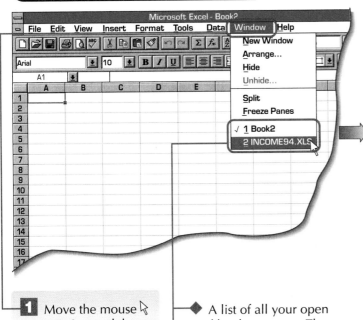

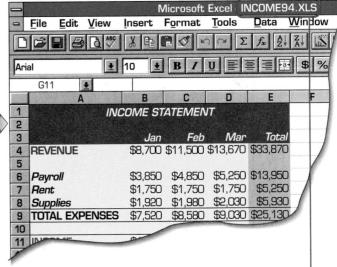

1 Move the mouse ⌖ over **Window** and then press the left button.

◆ A list of all your open workbooks appears. The current workbook displays a check mark (✓) beside its name.

2 Move the mouse ⌖ over the workbook you want to switch to (example: **INCOME94.XLS**) and then press the left button.

◆ The workbook appears.

◆ Excel displays the name of the workbook at the top of your screen.

ARRANGE OPEN WORKBOOKS

If you have several workbooks open, some of them may be hidden from view. You can use the Arrange command to view the contents of each workbook.

ARRANGE OPEN WORKBOOKS

Excel offers four ways to arrange open workbooks on your screen.

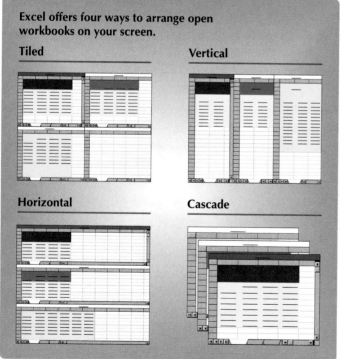

Tiled

Vertical

Horizontal

Cascade

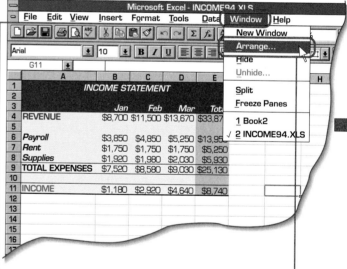

1 To arrange all of your open workbooks, move the mouse ⟨ over **Window** and then press the left button.

2 Move the mouse ⟨ over **Arrange** and then press the left button.

| Change Your Screen Display | Using Multiple Worksheets | **Using Multiple Workbooks** | Charting Data | Enhance a Chart | Drawing Objects | Manage Data in a List |

- Create a New Workbook
- Switch Between Workbooks
- **Arrange Open Workbooks**
- Close a Workbook
- Maximize a Workbook

You can easily move or copy data between open workbooks arranged on your screen.

1 Select the cells containing the data you want to move or copy to another workbook.

2 To move the data, move the mouse ⇧ over ✄ and then press the left button.

◆ To copy the data, move the mouse ⇧ over 📋 and then press the left button.

3 To select the workbook where you want to place the data, move the mouse ⇧ over the workbook and then press the left button.

4 Move the mouse ⊕ over the cell where you want to place the data and then press the left button. This cell will become the top left cell of the new location.

5 Move the mouse ⇧ over 📋 and then press the left button.

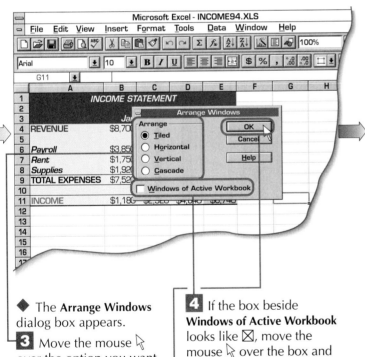

◆ The **Arrange Windows** dialog box appears.

3 Move the mouse ⇧ over the option you want to use (example: **Tiled**) and then press the left button (○ changes to ◉).

4 If the box beside **Windows of Active Workbook** looks like ⊠, move the mouse ⇧ over the box and then press the left button (⊠ changes to ☐).

5 Move the mouse ⇧ over **OK** and then press the left button.

◆ You can now view the contents of all your open workbooks.

◆ You can only work in the current workbook, which displays a highlighted title bar.

Note: To make another workbook current, move the mouse ⇧ anywhere over the workbook and then press the left button.

CLOSE A WORKBOOK ~MAXIMIZE A WORKBOOK

> When you finish working with a workbook, you can close it to remove the workbook from your screen.

CLOSE A WORKBOOK

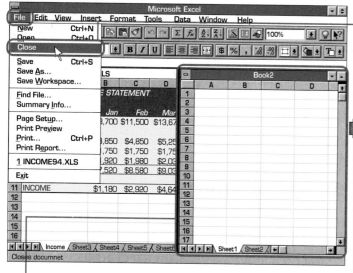

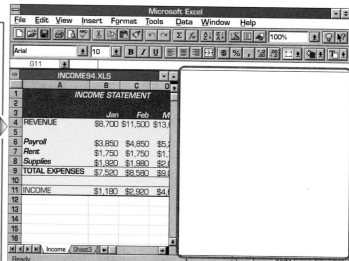

1 To select the workbook you want to close, move the mouse ⊕ anywhere over the workbook and then press the left button.

2 To save the workbook before closing, refer to page 28.

3 Move the mouse ⤡ over **File** and then press the left button.

4 Move the mouse ⤡ over **Close** and then press the left button.

◆ The workbook disappears from your screen.

| Change Your Screen Display | Using Multiple Worksheets | Using Multiple Workbooks | Charting Data | Enhance a Chart | Drawing Objects | Manage Data in a List |

- Create a New Workbook
- Switch Between Workbooks
- Arrange Open Workbooks
- **Close a Workbook**
- **Maximize a Workbook**

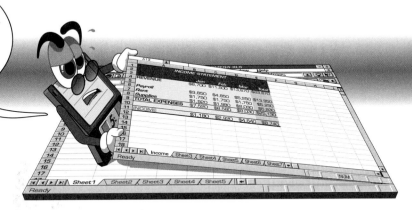

You can enlarge a workbook to fill your screen. This lets you view more of its contents.

MAXIMIZE A WORKBOOK

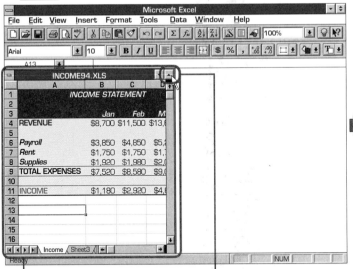

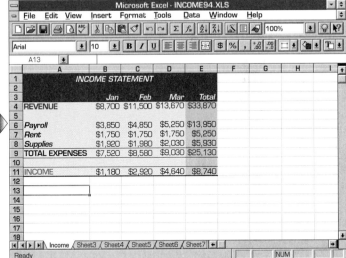

1 To select the workbook you want to maximize, move the mouse ⊹ anywhere over the workbook and then press the left button.

2 To maximize the workbook, move the mouse ⊳ over ▲ and then press the left button.

◆ The workbook enlarges to fill your screen.

CHARTING DATA

◆ In this chapter, you will learn how to create a chart using data from your worksheet. You will also learn how to make changes and print a chart.

INTRODUCTION

You can use a chart to visually display your worksheet data. Excel offers many different chart types.

PARTS OF A CHART

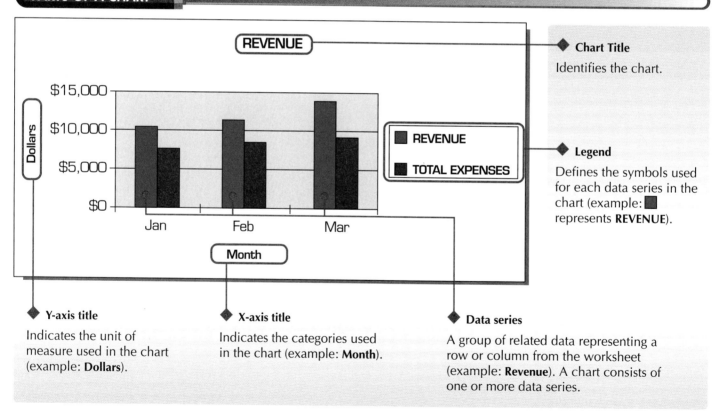

Chart Title
Identifies the chart.

Legend
Defines the symbols used for each data series in the chart (example: ■ represents **REVENUE**).

Y-axis title
Indicates the unit of measure used in the chart (example: **Dollars**).

X-axis title
Indicates the categories used in the chart (example: **Month**).

Data series
A group of related data representing a row or column from the worksheet (example: **Revenue**). A chart consists of one or more data series.

WORKING WITH EXCEL

Change Your Screen Display	Using Multiple Worksheets	Using Multiple Workbooks	Charting Data	Enhance a Chart	Drawing Objects	Manage Data in a List

Charting Data

- **Introduction**
- Create a Chart
- Create a Chart on a Chart Sheet
- Move a Chart

- Size a Chart
- Add a Data Series to a Chart
- Add Titles to a Chart
- Print a Chart

CHART TYPES

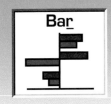

AREA*

Each line represents a data series. The area below each line is filled in. This is useful for showing the amount of change in values over time (example: sales figures for the last five years).

PIE*

This chart shows each value in a data series as a piece of a pie. A pie chart can only display one data series at a time. This is useful for showing percentages (example: January sales as a percentage of sales for the year).

BAR*

Each horizontal bar represents a value in a data series. This chart shows differences between values (example: a comparison of revenue and expenses for each month in a year).

DOUGHNUT

This chart is similar to a pie chart except it can display more than one data series at a time. Each ring represents a data series.

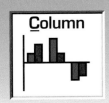

COLUMN*

This chart is similar to a bar chart, except vertical bars represent the values in a data series.

RADAR

This chart represents each data series as a line around a central point (example: each month is an axis, the distance from the center point shows the sales for the month).

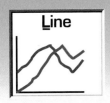

LINE*

Each line represents a data series. This is useful for showing the rate of change in values over time.

XY (SCATTER)

This chart shows the relationship between two or more data series (example: relationship between education and life-time earnings).

* **Excel also offers these chart types in 3-D.**

CREATE A CHART

You can create a chart directly from your worksheet data. Excel provides a ChartWizard to lead you through each step.

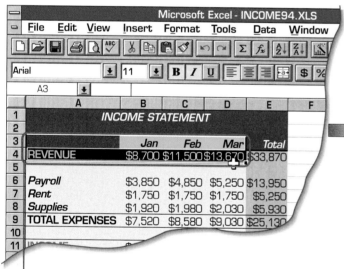

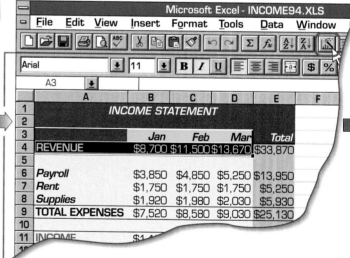

1 Select the cells containing the data you want to chart, including the row and column headings.

Note: To select cells, refer to page 12.

2 To display the chart on the current worksheet, move the mouse ⤢ over 📊 and then press the left button (⤢ changes to ⁺₍ₗₗ₎).

Note: To display the chart on a separate chart sheet, refer to page 178.

172

Tip

You can display your chart in one of two locations.

◆ Display the chart
and data on the same
worksheet. To do this,
perform the steps below.

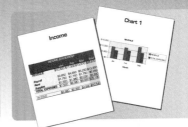

◆ Display the chart
and data on separate
sheets. To do this, refer
to page 178.

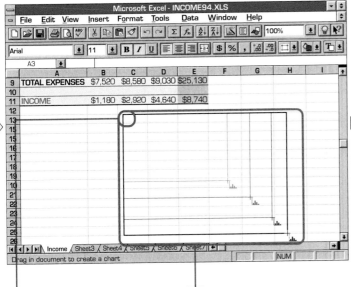

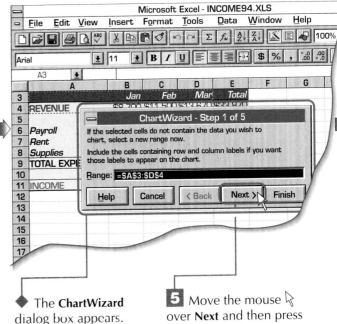

3 Move the mouse +⬛
over the location where you
want the top left corner of
the chart to appear.

4 Press and hold down the
left button as you drag the
mouse +⬛ until the rectangle
displays the size of the chart
you want. Then release the
button.

◆ The **ChartWizard**
dialog box appears.

5 Move the mouse ⬉
over **Next** and then press
the left button.

Note: To continue creating a chart,
refer to the next page.

CREATE A CHART

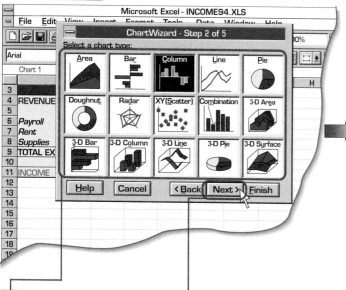

6 To select a chart type, move the mouse ⤢ over the type you want to use (example: **Column**) and then press the left button.

7 To display the next step, move the mouse ⤢ over **Next** and then press the left button.

8 To select a format for the chart type you selected, move the mouse ⤢ over the format you want to use (example: **6**) and then press the left button.

9 To display the next step, move the mouse ⤢ over **Next** and then press the left button.

The ChartWizard dialog box offers several buttons that you can use while creating your chart.

| **Help** | To display Help information, move the mouse ⤢ over **Help** and then press the left button. |

| **Cancel** | To cancel the creation of the chart, move the mouse ⤢ over **Cancel** and then press the left button. |

| **‹Back** | To return to the previous step, move the mouse ⤢ over **Back** and then press the left button. |

STEP 4 · SPECIFY THE DATA SERIES, AXIS LABELS AND LEGEND TEXT

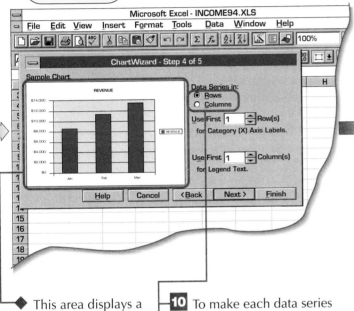

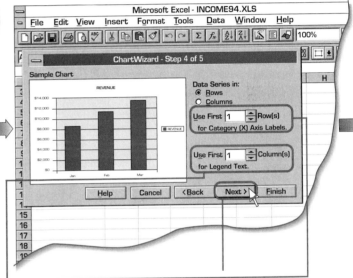

◆ This area displays a sample of your chart.

Note: The options in this dialog box depend on the chart type you selected in step 6.

10 To make each data series represent a row of data from your worksheet, move the mouse ⌖ over **Rows** and then press the left button.

◆ To make each data series represent a column of data from your worksheet, move the mouse ⌖ over **Columns** and then press the left button.

11 To change the number of rows from your worksheet that contain the category (x) axis labels, press **Tab** and then type the number of rows.

12 To change the number of columns from your worksheet that contain the legend text, press **Tab** and then type the number of columns.

13 To display the next step, move the mouse ⌖ over **Next** and then press the left button.

Note: To continue creating a chart, refer to the next page.

175

CREATE A CHART

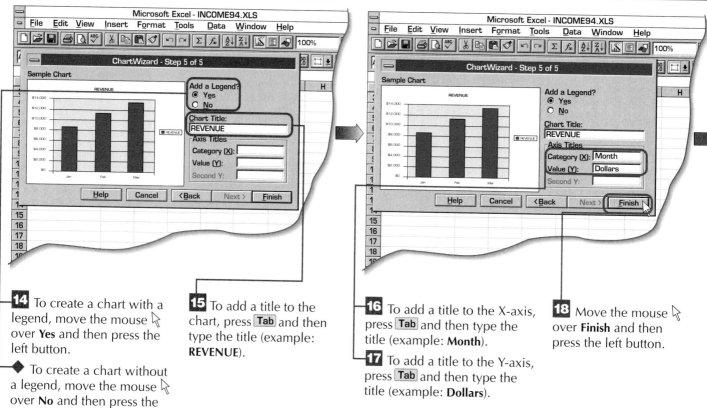

14 To create a chart with a legend, move the mouse ⟍ over **Yes** and then press the left button.

◆ To create a chart without a legend, move the mouse ⟍ over **No** and then press the left button.

15 To add a title to the chart, press **Tab** and then type the title (example: **REVENUE**).

16 To add a title to the X-axis, press **Tab** and then type the title (example: **Month**).

17 To add a title to the Y-axis, press **Tab** and then type the title (example: **Dollars**).

18 Move the mouse ⟍ over **Finish** and then press the left button.

Change
Your Screen
Display

Using
Multiple
Worksheets

Using
Multiple
Workbooks

Charting
Data

Enhance a
Chart

Drawing
Objects

Manage
Data in a List

• Introduction
• **Create a Chart**
• Create a Chart on a Chart Sheet
• Move a Chart

• Size a Chart
• Add a Data Series to a Chart
• Add Titles to a Chart
• Print a Chart

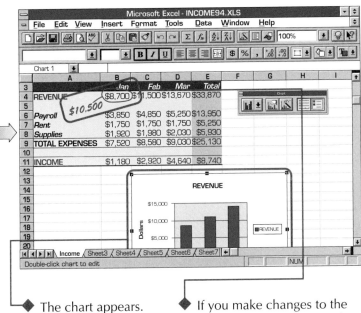

◆ The chart appears.

◆ If you make changes to the data in your worksheet, Excel automatically updates the chart to reflect the changes.

*Note: In this example, the data in **B4** changes from **$8,700** to **$10,500**.*

◆ The changes made to the data in your worksheet appear in the chart.

◆ To view your entire chart, move the mouse ⌖ over ⬇ and then press the left button.

To save your chart, you must save the workbook. For more information, refer to page 28.

CREATE A CHART ON A CHART SHEET

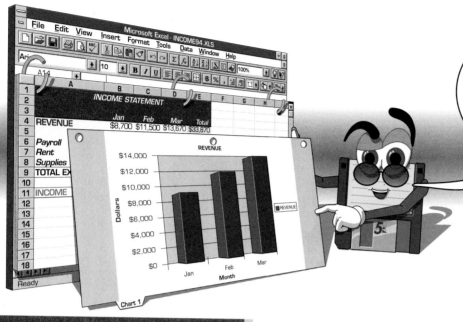

You can create a chart on a chart sheet in your workbook. This is useful if you want to display the chart and data separately.

CREATE A CHART ON A CHART SHEET

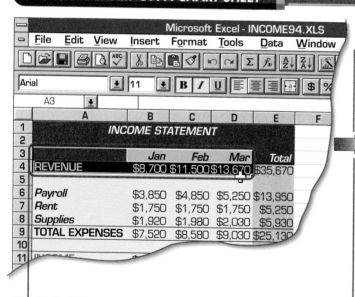

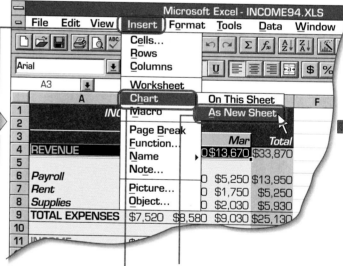

1 Select the cells containing the data you want to chart, including the row and column headings.

Note: To select cells, refer to page 12.

2 Move the mouse ⊠ over **Insert** and then press the left button.

3 Move the mouse ⊠ over **Chart** and then press the left button.

4 Move the mouse ⊠ over **As New Sheet** and then press the left button.

178

| Change Your Screen Display | Using Multiple Worksheets | Using Multiple Workbooks | Charting Data | Enhance a Chart | Drawing Objects | Manage Data in a List |

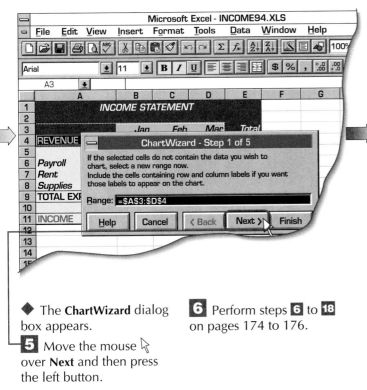

Tip

Creating a chart on a separate chart sheet is similar to placing a new sheet of paper in a three-ring binder.

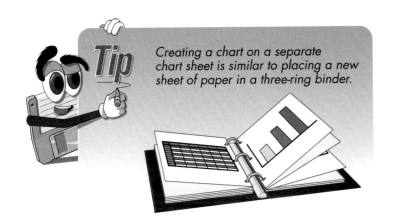

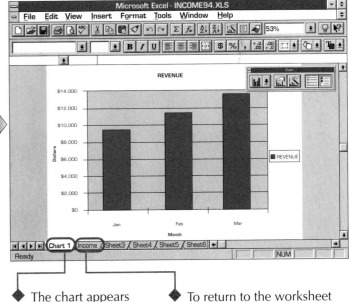

◆ The **ChartWizard** dialog box appears.

5 Move the mouse ⬚ over **Next** and then press the left button.

6 Perform steps **6** to **18** on pages 174 to 176.

◆ The chart appears on a chart sheet (example: **Chart 1**).

◆ To return to the worksheet containing your data, move the mouse ⬚ over the worksheet tab (example: **Income**) and then press the left button.

MOVE A CHART   SIZE A CHART

After you create a chart, you can move it to a more suitable location in your worksheet. You can also change the overall size of the chart.

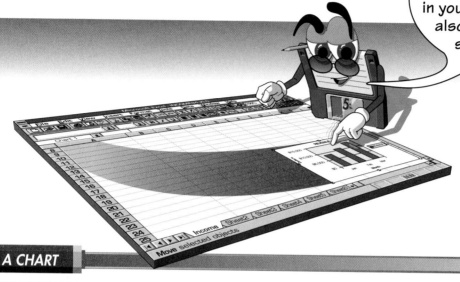

MOVE A CHART

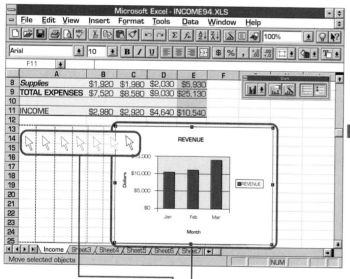

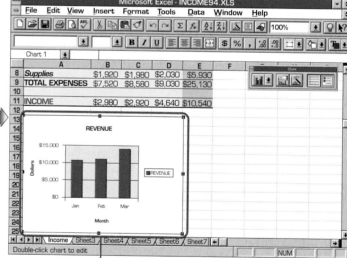

1 To deselect a chart, move the mouse ⊕ over any cell outside the chart and then press the left button.

2 To move a chart, move the mouse ⊾ anywhere over the chart.

3 Press and hold down the left button as you drag the chart to a new location.

◆ A dotted rectangular box shows the new location.

4 Release the button and the chart moves to the new location.

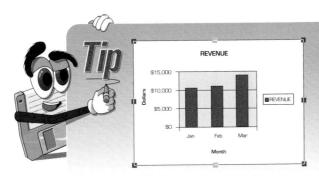

You can change the size of a chart using any handle around the chart.

You can use these handles to change the height of a chart.

You can use these handles to change the width of a chart.

You can use these handles to change the height and width of a chart at the same time.

SIZE A CHART

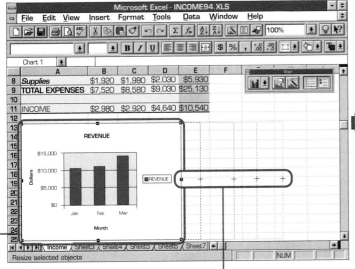

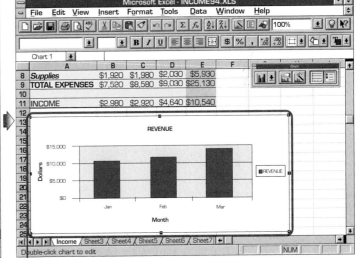

1 To deselect a chart, move the mouse over any cell outside the chart and then press the left button.

2 Move the mouse anywhere over the chart and then press the left button. Handles (■) appear around the chart.

3 Move the mouse over one of the handles (■) and changes to ↔.

4 Press and hold down the left button as you drag the chart to the new size.

◆ A dotted rectangular box shows the new size.

5 Release the button and the chart displays the new size.

181

ADD A DATA SERIES TO A CHART

After you create a chart, you can easily add another data series.

ADD A DATA SERIES TO A CHART

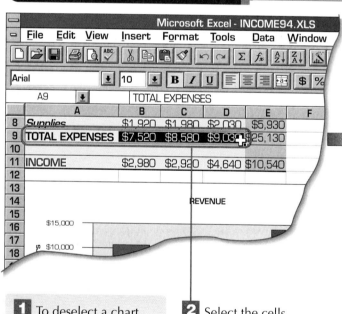

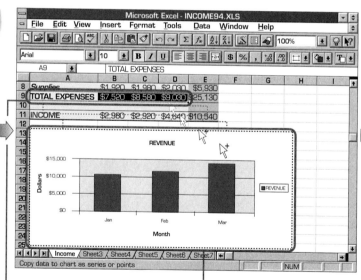

1 To deselect a chart, move the mouse ⊹ over any cell outside the chart and then press the left button.

2 Select the cells containing the data you want to add to the chart.

Note: To select cells, refer to page 12.

3 Move the mouse ⊹ over a border of the cells you selected (⊹ changes to ⇗) and then press and hold down the left button.

4 Still holding down the button, drag the mouse ⇗ anywhere over the chart. Then release the button.

182

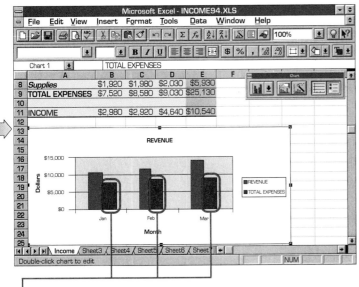

◆ The chart displays the new data series.

ADD A DATA SERIES TO A CHART SHEET

1 Select the cells containing the data you want to add to the chart.

2 To make a copy of the data, move the mouse over 🗐 and then press the left button.

3 Move the mouse over the tab of the chart sheet where you want to add the data and then press the left button.

4 To add the data to the chart, move the mouse over 🗐 and then press the left button.

After you create a chart, you can add a chart title and axis titles. Titles make your data more meaningful.

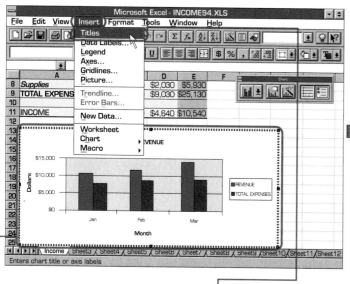

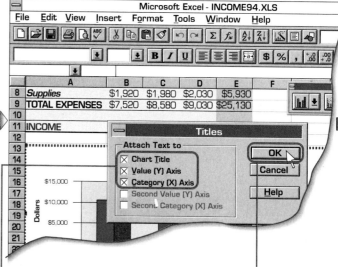

◆ You must first select the chart you want to change. A selected chart displays a colored border.

1 To select a chart, move the mouse ⬚ anywhere over the chart and then quickly press the left button twice.

2 Move the mouse ⬚ over **Insert** and then press the left button.

3 Move the mouse ⬚ over **Titles** and then press the left button.

◆ The **Titles** dialog box appears.

4 To add a title, move the mouse ⬚ over the title you want to add and then press the left button.

Note: ⊠ indicates a title will appear.
☐ indicates a title will not appear.

5 When you have selected all the titles you want to add, move the mouse ⬚ over **OK** and then press the left button.

Tip

You can change a title after adding it to your chart.

◆ You must first select the chart you want to change. A selected chart displays a colored border.

1 To select a chart, move the mouse ⏵ anywhere over the chart and then quickly press the left button twice.

2 To edit a title, perform steps **6** to **8** below.

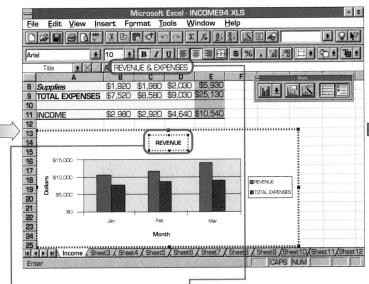

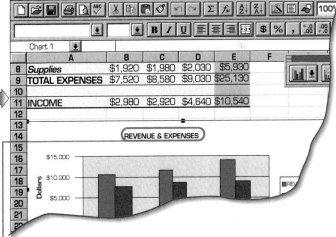

◆ The titles you selected appear in your chart.

*Note: If you add a new axis title, your chart will display the letter **x** or **y** as a temporary title.*

6 To select a title you want to edit, move the mouse ⏵ over the title and then press the left button. A border appears around the title.

7 Type the new title.

◆ The formula bar displays the text you type.

8 Press **Enter** on your keyboard to display the title in the chart.

Note: To deselect the title, move the mouse ⏵ anywhere outside the title area and then press the left button.

You can print your chart with the worksheet data or on its own page.

PRINT A CHART WITH WORKSHEET DATA

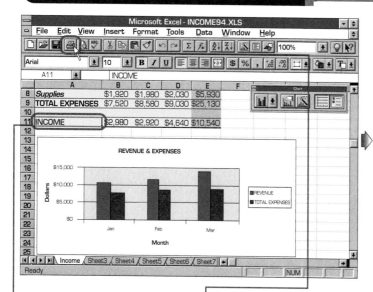

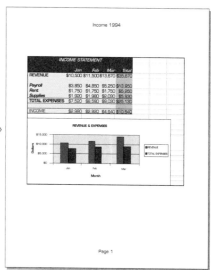

1 Move the mouse ⊹ over any cell outside the chart and then press the left button.

2 Move the mouse ▷ over 🖨 and then press the left button.

Note: For more information on printing, refer to page 122.

Note: A colorful chart can be difficult to read when printed on a black and white printer. To avoid problems, you can print the chart in black and white. For more information, refer to page 126.

PRINT A CHART ON A CHART SHEET

1 To display the chart on your screen, move the mouse ⬚ over the chart tab and then press the left button.

2 Move the mouse ⬚ over 🖨 and then press the left button.

PRINT A CHART ON ITS OWN PAGE

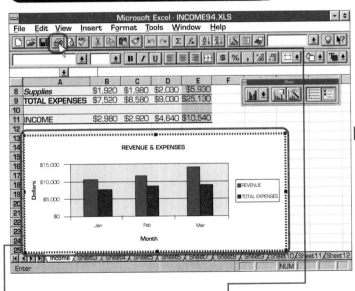

◆ To print a chart on its own page, you must first select the chart. A selected chart displays a colored border.

1 To select a chart, move the mouse ⬚ anywhere over the chart and then quickly press the left button twice.

2 Move the mouse ⬚ over 🖨 and then press the left button.

187

Overview

ENHANCE A CHART

Change Chart Type

Format a Chart Automatically

Format a 3-D Chart

Add Color to a Chart

Format Text in a Chart

◆ In this chapter, you will learn how to enhance a chart by changing the chart type, adding color and formatting text.

CHANGE CHART TYPE

After creating a chart, you can select a new type that will better suit your data.

CHANGE CHART TYPE

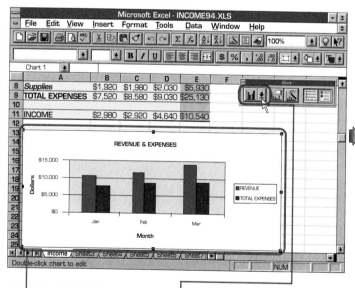

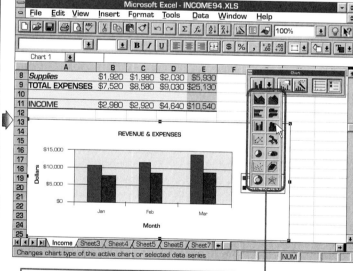

1 Move the mouse ⤢ anywhere over the chart and then press the left button.

2 Move the mouse ⤢ over ⬇ on the **Chart** toolbar and then press the left button.

Note: To display the **Chart** toolbar, refer to page 140.

◆ The available chart types appear.

3 Move the mouse ⤢ over the chart type you want to use and then press the left button.

190

Change
Your Screen
Display

Using
Multiple
Worksheets

Using
Multiple
Workbooks

Charting
Data

Enhance a
Chart

Drawing
Objects

Manage
Data in a List

- **Change Chart Type**
- Format a Chart Automatically
- Format a 3-D Chart
- Add Color to a Chart
- Format Text in a Chart

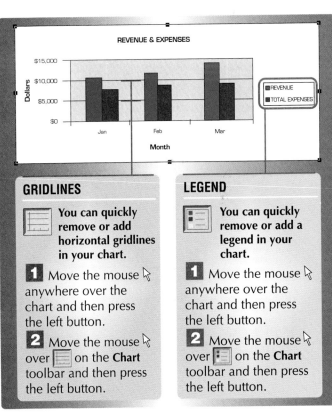

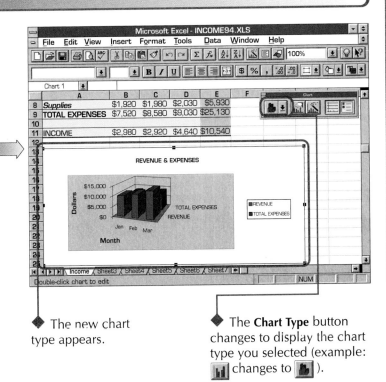

◆ The new chart
type appears.

◆ The **Chart Type** button
changes to display the chart
type you selected (example:
📊 changes to 📊).

GRIDLINES

You can quickly
remove or add
horizontal gridlines
in your chart.

1 Move the mouse ⌖
anywhere over the
chart and then press
the left button.

2 Move the mouse ⌖
over 📄 on the **Chart**
toolbar and then press
the left button.

LEGEND

You can quickly
remove or add a
legend in your
chart.

1 Move the mouse ⌖
anywhere over the
chart and then press
the left button.

2 Move the mouse ⌖
over 📄 on the **Chart**
toolbar and then press
the left button.

FORMAT A CHART AUTOMATICALLY

The AutoFormat feature provides a selection of formats that you can choose from to enhance the appearance of your chart.

FORMAT A CHART AUTOMATICALLY

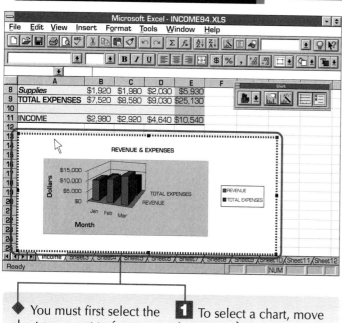

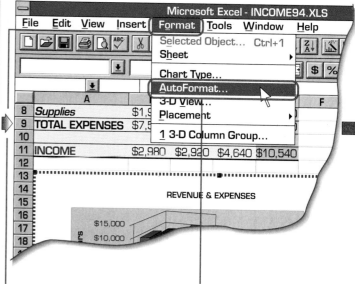

◆ You must first select the chart you want to format. A selected chart displays a colored border.

1 To select a chart, move the mouse anywhere over the chart and then quickly press the left button twice.

2 Move the mouse over **Format** and then press the left button.

3 Move the mouse over **AutoFormat** and then press the left button.

192

Change Your Screen Display	Using Multiple Worksheets	Using Multiple Workbooks	Charting Data	**Enhance a Chart**	Drawing Objects	Manage Data in a List

- Change Chart Type
- **Format a Chart Automatically**
- Format a 3-D Chart
- Add Color to a Chart
- Format Text in a Chart

Tip

If you are not satisfied with the results of the AutoFormat feature, you can undo the changes.

1 To undo the AutoFormat immediately after applying the format, move the mouse ⬚ over ◄ and then press the left button.

Note: For more information on the Undo feature, refer to page 43.

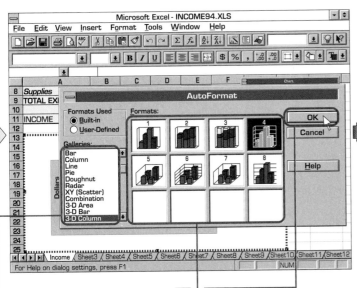

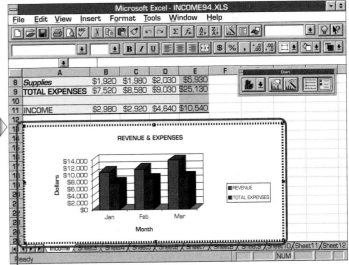

◆ The **AutoFormat** dialog box appears.

4 Move the mouse ⬚ over the chart type you want to use (example: **3-D Column**) and then press the left button.

5 Move the mouse ⬚ over the format you want to use (example: **4**) and then press the left button.

6 Move the mouse ⬚ over **OK** and then press the left button.

◆ Your chart displays the new formats.

193

FORMAT A
3-D CHART

You can change the rotation and elevation of a 3-D chart.

FORMAT A 3-D CHART

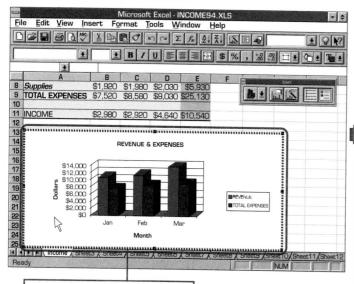

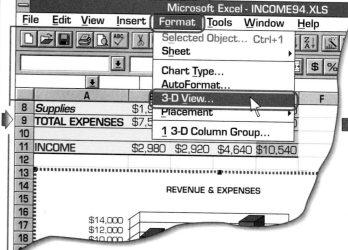

◆ You must first select the chart you want to format. A selected chart displays a colored border.

1 To select a chart, move the mouse ↖ anywhere over the chart and then quickly press the left button.

2 Move the mouse ↖ over **Format** and then press the left button.

3 Move the mouse ↖ over **3-D View** and then press the left button.

Note: The **3-D View** command is only available if your chart is displayed in 3-D. To display your chart in 3-D, refer to page 192.

◆ The **Format 3-D View** dialog box appears.

Change Your Screen Display	Using Multiple Worksheets	Using Multiple Workbooks	Charting Data	Enhance a Chart	Drawing Objects	Manage Data in a List

- Change Chart Type
- Format a Chart Automatically
- **Format a 3-D Chart**
- Add Color to a Chart
- Format Text in a Chart

Tip

After changing the format of a 3-D chart, you can return the chart to its original format.

1 Perform steps **1** to **3** below.

2 Move the mouse ⃗ over **Default** and then press the left button.

3 Move the mouse ⃗ over **OK** and then press the left button.

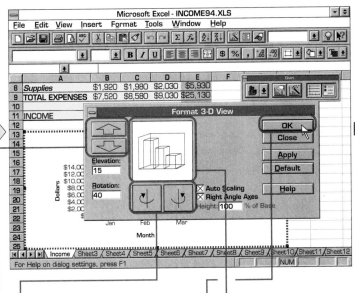

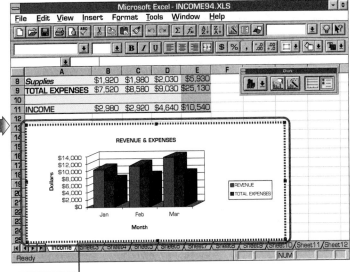

4 To change the rotation of the 3-D chart, move the mouse ⃗ over one of these arrows and then press the left button.

5 To change the elevation of the 3-D chart, move the mouse ⃗ over one of these arrows and then press the left button.

◆ This area displays a sample of the chart.

6 Move the mouse ⃗ over **OK** and then press the left button.

◆ Your chart displays the new formats.

ADD COLOR TO A CHART

You can add color to any part of your chart. Color can make your chart more attractive.

ADD COLOR TO A CHART

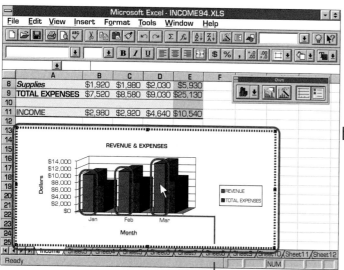

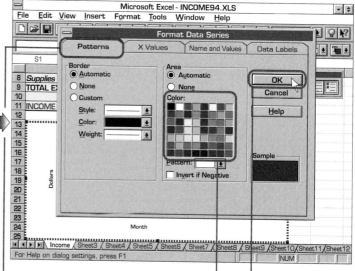

◆ You must first select the chart you want to change. A selected chart displays a colored border.

1 To select a chart, move the mouse anywhere over the chart and then quickly press the left button twice.

2 Move the mouse over the area of the chart where you want to display a new color and then quickly press the left button twice.

◆ A formatting dialog box appears.

Note: The dialog box that appears depends on the area you selected in step **2**.

3 Move the mouse over the **Patterns** tab and then press the left button.

4 Move the mouse over the color you want to use and then press the left button.

5 Move the mouse over **OK** and then press the left button.

Change Your Screen Display	Using Multiple Worksheets	Using Multiple Workbooks	Charting Data	**Enhance a Chart**	Drawing Objects	Manage Data in a List

- Change Chart Type
- Format a Chart Automatically
- Format a 3-D Chart
- **Add Color to a Chart**
- Format Text in a Chart

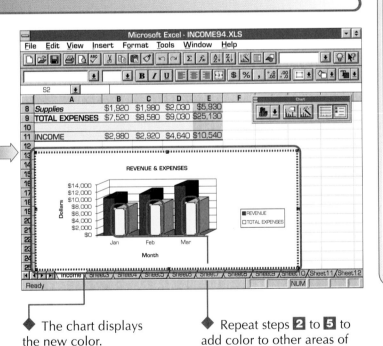

◆ The chart displays the new color.

◆ Repeat steps **2** to **5** to add color to other areas of your chart.

SHORTCUT

To quickly add color to a chart:

◆ You must first select the chart you want to change. A selected chart displays a colored border.

1 To select a chart, move the mouse ⟍ anywhere over the chart and then quickly press the left button twice.

2 Move the mouse ⟍ over the text or area of the chart where you want to display the new color and then press the left button.

3 To change the color of text, move the mouse ⟍ over ▾ beside [T] and then press the left button.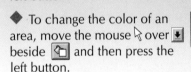

◆ To change the color of an area, move the mouse ⟍ over ▾ beside [◇] and then press the left button.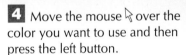

4 Move the mouse ⟍ over the color you want to use and then press the left button.

197

FORMAT TEXT IN A CHART

You can change the design and size of text in your chart. This will improve the overall appearance of the chart.

FORMAT TEXT IN A CHART

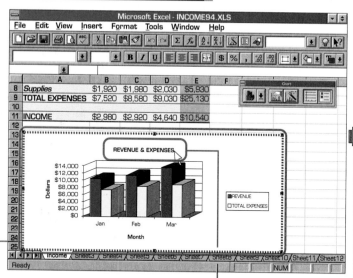

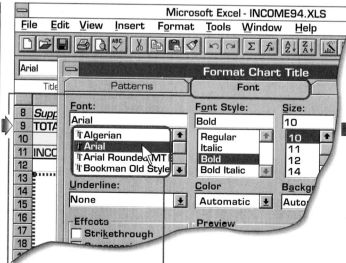

◆ You must first select the chart you want to change. A selected chart displays a colored border.

1 To select a chart, move the mouse ⟨ anywhere over the chart and then quickly press the left button twice.

2 Move the mouse ⟨ over the text you want to format and then quickly press the left button twice.

◆ A formatting dialog box appears.

Note: The dialog box that appears depends on the text you selected in step 2.

3 Move the mouse ⟨ over the **Font** tab and then press the left button.

4 Move the mouse ⟨ over the font you want to use (example: **Arial**) and then press the left button.

Note: To view all of the available fonts, use the scroll bar. For more information, refer to page 21.

Change
Your Screen
Display

Using
Multiple
Worksheets

Using
Multiple
Workbooks

Charting
Data

Enhance a
Chart

Drawing
Objects

Manage
Data in a List

- Change Chart Type
- Format a Chart Automatically
- Format a 3-D Chart
- Add Color to a Chart
- **Format Text in a Chart**

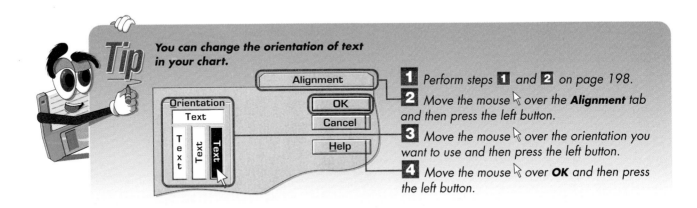

Tip

You can change the orientation of text in your chart.

1 Perform steps **1** and **2** on page 198.

2 Move the mouse ⓘ over the **Alignment** tab and then press the left button.

3 Move the mouse ⓘ over the orientation you want to use and then press the left button.

4 Move the mouse ⓘ over **OK** and then press the left button.

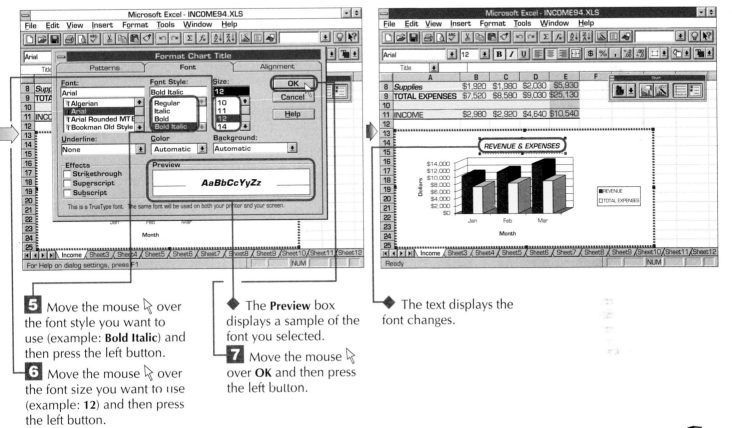

5 Move the mouse ⓘ over the font style you want to use (example: **Bold Italic**) and then press the left button.

6 Move the mouse ⓘ over the font size you want to use (example: **12**) and then press the left button.

◆ The **Preview** box displays a sample of the font you selected.

7 Move the mouse ⓘ over **OK** and then press the left button.

◆ The text displays the font changes.

199

verview

DRAWING OBJECTS

Add a Text Box
Draw Shapes and Lines
Size an Object
Move an Object

◆ In this chapter, you will learn how to emphasize data by adding objects to your worksheet and chart.

ADD A TEXT BOX

You can add a text box to your chart or worksheet to provide additional information about your data.

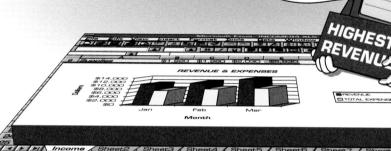

ADD A TEXT BOX

You can place a text box in one of two locations.

On your worksheet

On your chart

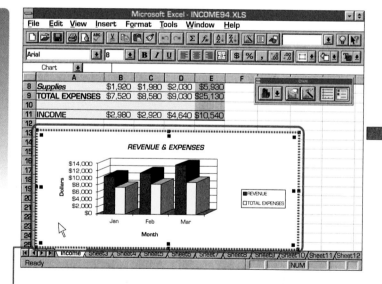

◆ To add a text box to a chart, you must first select the chart. A selected chart displays a colored border.

1 To select a chart, move the mouse ⌖ anywhere over the chart and then quickly press the left button twice.

◆ To add a text box to a worksheet, move the mouse ⌐┘ over any cell in the worksheet and then press the left button.

| Change Your Screen Display | Using Multiple Worksheets | Using Multiple Workbooks | Charting Data | Enhance a Chart | Drawing Objects | Manage Data in a List |

• Add a Text Box
• Draw Shapes and Lines
• Size an Object
• Move an Object

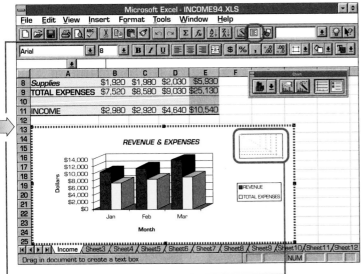

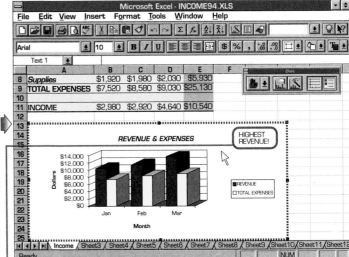

2 Move the mouse ☐ over 🖿 and then press the left button.

3 Move the mouse **+** over the area where you want to display the top left corner of the text box.

4 Press and hold down the left button as you drag the mouse **+** until the box displays the desired size. Then release the button.

5 Type the text you want to appear in the text box.

6 When you finish typing the text, move the mouse ☐ anywhere outside the text box area and then press the left button.

DRAW SHAPES AND LINES

You can draw shapes and lines to emphasize specific areas of your chart or worksheet.

You can place a shape or line in one of two locations.

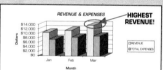

On your worksheet

On your chart

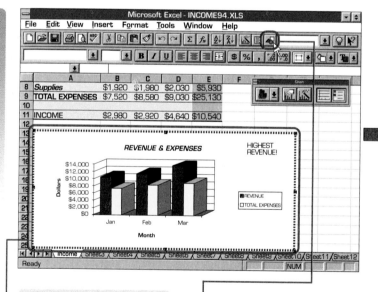

◆ To add a shape or line to a chart, you must first select the chart. A selected chart displays a colored border.

1 To select a chart, move the mouse ☖ anywhere over the chart and then quickly press the left button twice.

◆ To add a shape or line to a worksheet, move the mouse ⊹ over any cell in the worksheet and then press the left button.

2 To display the **Drawing** toolbar, move the mouse ☖ over ◨ and then press the left button.

Change Your Screen Display | Using Multiple Worksheets | Using Multiple Workbooks | Charting Data | Enhance a Chart | **Drawing Objects** | Manage Data in a List

- Add a Text Box
- **Draw Shapes and Lines**
- Size an Object
- Move an Object

You can use these drawing tools to enhance your chart or worksheet.

Use this button to draw a straight line

Use these buttons to draw an arc

Use these buttons to draw a rectangle or square

Use this button to draw an arrow

Use these buttons to draw an ellipse or circle

Use this button to draw a wavy line

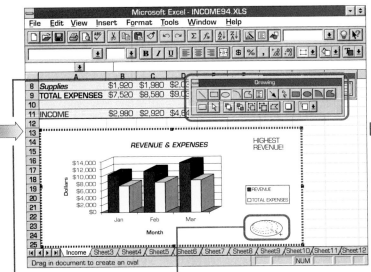

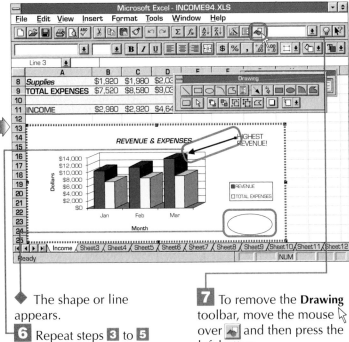

◆ The **Drawing** toolbar appears.

3 Move the mouse over the shape or line you want to draw and then press the left button.

4 Move the mouse + over the area where you want the shape or line to begin.

5 Press and hold down the left button as you drag the mouse + until the shape or line displays the desired size. Then release the button.

◆ The shape or line appears.

6 Repeat steps **3** to **5** for each object you want to draw.

7 To remove the **Drawing** toolbar, move the mouse over and then press the left button.

SIZE AN OBJECT   MOVE AN OBJECT

You can easily change the size or location of an object.

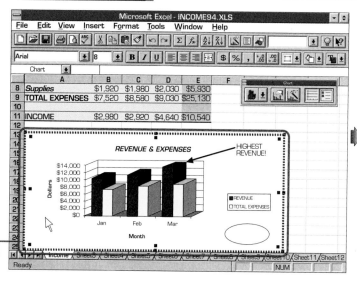

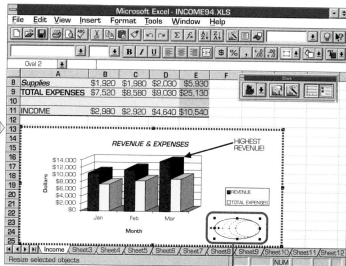

◆ To size an object in a chart, you must first select the chart. A selected chart displays a colored border.

1 To select a chart, move the mouse ⩗ anywhere over the chart and then quickly press the left button twice.

◆ To size an object in a worksheet, move the mouse ⌐ over any cell in the worksheet and then press the left button.

2 Move the mouse ⩗ over an edge of the object you want to size and then press the left button. Boxes (■) appear around the object.

3 Move the mouse ⩗ over one of the boxes (⩗ changes to ↔) and then press and hold down the left button.

4 Still holding down the left button, drag the mouse + until the object displays the size you want.

Change
Your Screen
Display

Using
Multiple
Worksheets

Using
Multiple
Workbooks

Charting
Data

Enhance a
Chart

Drawing
Objects

Manage
Data in a List

• Add a Text Box
• Draw Shapes and Lines
• **Size an Object**
• **Move an Object**

DELETE AN OBJECT

1 To select the object you want to delete, perform steps **1** and **2** on page 206.

2 Press **Delete** on your keyboard.

MOVE AN OBJECT

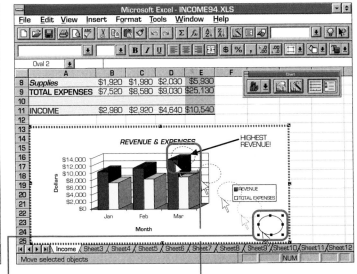

5 Release the left button and the object displays the new size.

1 To select the object you want to move, perform steps **1** and **2** on page 206.

2 Move the mouse ⟍ over an edge of the object (not a box ■) and then press and hold down the left button.

3 Still holding down the left button, drag the mouse ⟍ where you want to place the object.

4 Release the left button and the object appears in the new location.

Note: You cannot move an object on a chart to a location outside the chart area.

Overview

MANAGE DATA IN A LIST

◆ In this chapter, you will learn how to manage a large collection of information.

Excel provides powerful tools for organizing, managing, sorting and retrieving data from a large collection of information.

STORE DATA

You can keep your data in an organized and up-to-date list. For example, you can create a list to keep track of the number of units each employee sells per month.

SORT DATA

You can change the order that data appears in a list. Excel lets you sort data by letter, number or date. For example, you can alphabetically sort the names of all your employees.

FIND DATA

You can easily find specific data in a large list. You can then compare and analyze the data. For example, you can search for the names of the employees who sold more than 1000 units last month.

CREATE A LIST

You can create a list in a worksheet to store a collection of related data.

RECORDS

A record is a group of related data in a list (example: all the information for one employee).

FIELD NAMES

A field name is a title for one category of data in a list (example: **Last Name**).

Last Name	Devries
First Name	Betty
Product	A
Units Sold	685

CREATE A LIST

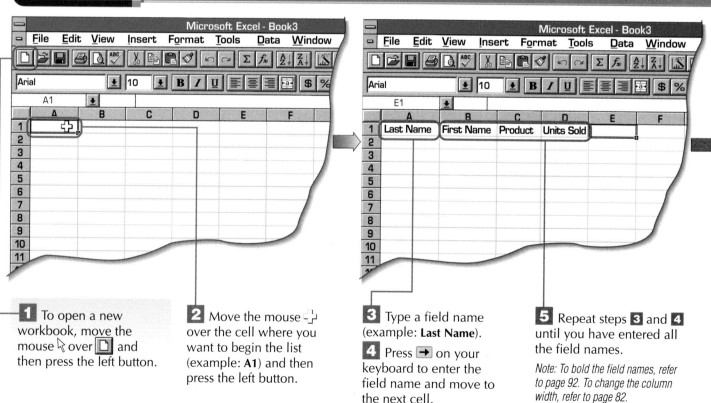

1 To open a new workbook, move the mouse ⟍ over ▯ and then press the left button.

2 Move the mouse ⊹ over the cell where you want to begin the list (example: **A1**) and then press the left button.

3 Type a field name (example: **Last Name**).

4 Press → on your keyboard to enter the field name and move to the next cell.

5 Repeat steps **3** and **4** until you have entered all the field names.

Note: To bold the field names, refer to page 92. To change the column width, refer to page 82.

212

- Introduction
- **Create a List**
- Find Data in a List
- Filter a List
- Sort Data
- Add Subtotals to a List
- Hide or Display Subtotaled Data

	A	B	C	D
1	Last Name	First Name	Product	Units Sold
2	Devries	Betty	A	685
3	Smith	Monica	C	934
4	Appleton	Jill	A	812
5	Smith	Rob	C	1625
6	Ross	Albert	B	598
7	Zellers	Gavin	A	632
8	Linton	Mark	C	795
9	Matwey	Jennifer	B	956
10	Smith	Carol	A	578

◆ The first row of your list contains the **field names**.

◆ Each of the following rows contains one **record**.

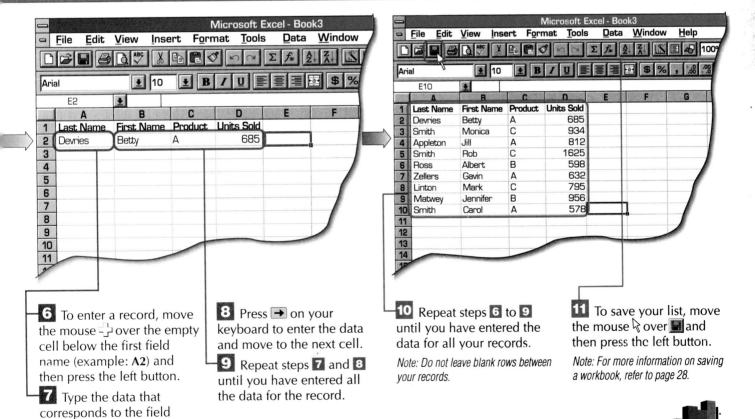

6 To enter a record, move the mouse ⬚ over the empty cell below the first field name (example: A2) and then press the left button.

7 Type the data that corresponds to the field name (example: **Devries**).

8 Press ➡ on your keyboard to enter the data and move to the next cell.

9 Repeat steps **7** and **8** until you have entered all the data for the record.

10 Repeat steps **6** to **9** until you have entered the data for all your records.

Note: Do not leave blank rows between your records.

11 To save your list, move the mouse ▷ over 🖫 and then press the left button.

Note: For more information on saving a workbook, refer to page 28.

213

FIND DATA
IN A LIST

You can search
for specific records in
your list. Excel displays
one matching record
at a time.

FIND DATA IN A LIST

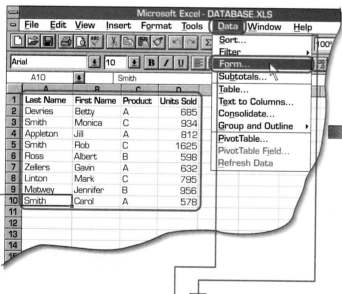

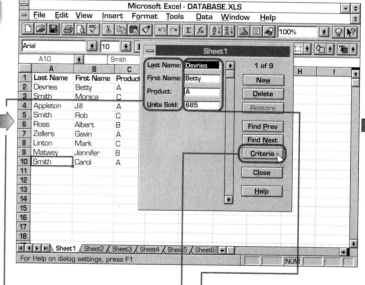

**In this example, Excel will
find all records with the last
name Smith.**

1 Move the mouse over any cell in the list and then press the left button.

2 Move the mouse over **Data** and then press the left button.

3 Move the mouse over **Form** and then press the left button.

◆ The **Sheet1** dialog box appears.

◆ This area displays the field names from your list.

◆ These boxes display the data for the first record in your list.

4 To specify the data you want to find, move the mouse over **Criteria** and then press the left button.

WORKING WITH EXCEL

| Change Your Screen Display | Using Multiple Worksheets | Using Multiple Workbooks | Charting Data | Enhance a Chart | Drawing Objects | Manage Data in a List |

- Introduction
- Create a List
- **Find Data in a List**
- Filter a List
- Sort Data
- Add Subtotals to a List
- Hide or Display Subtotaled Data

OPERATORS

= finds all records that match   >= finds all records that match or are higher

> finds all records that are higher   <= finds all records that match or are lower

< finds all records that are lower   <> finds all records that do not match

Note: 1 is lower than 2, A is lower than B.

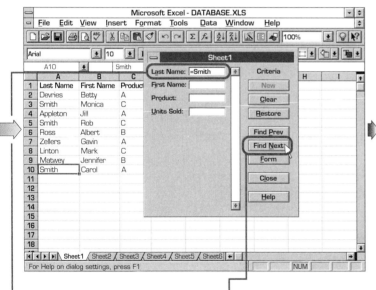

5 Move the mouse ⊥ over the box beside the field name you want to use in the search (example: **Last Name**) and then press the left button.

6 Type the operator followed by the data you want to find (example: **=Smith**).

7 To search forward through the list, move the mouse � over **Find Next** and then press the left button.

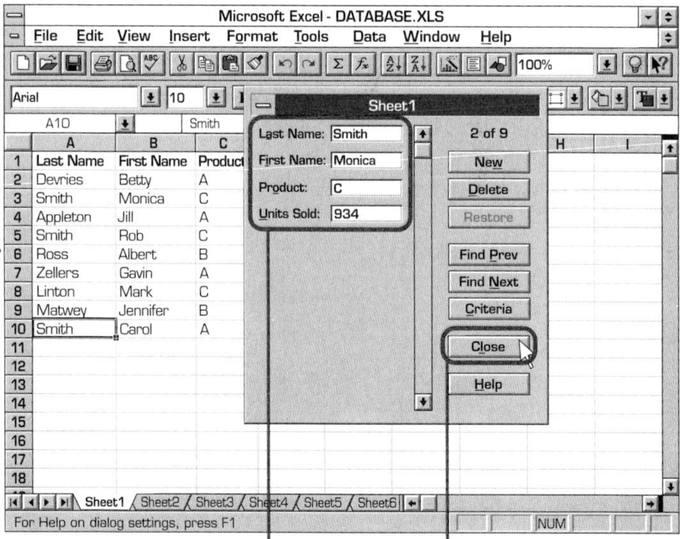

◆ The first matching record appears.

8 To display the next matching record, repeat step **7**.

*Note: To search backward through the list, move the mouse � over **Find Prev** and then press the left button.*

9 When you finish viewing the matching records, move the mouse � over **Close** and then press the left button.

215

FILTER A LIST

You can use the AutoFilter feature to narrow your list and display only the records containing the data you specify. This lets you easily compare data by hiding the records you do not need.

FILTER A LIST

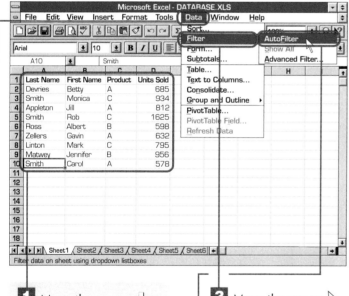

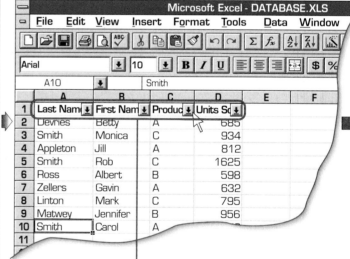

1 Move the mouse ⊕ over any cell in the list and then press the left button.

2 Move the mouse ⊳ over **Data** and then press the left button.

3 Move the mouse ⊳ over **Filter** and then press the left button.

4 Move the mouse ⊳ over **AutoFilter** and then press the left button.

◆ A ▾ appears beside each field name in your list.

5 Move the mouse ⊳ over ▾ in the column you want to use to filter the list (example: **Product**) and then press the left button.

UNFILTER A LIST

1 To turn off the AutoFilter feature and display your entire list, perform steps **2** to **4** below.

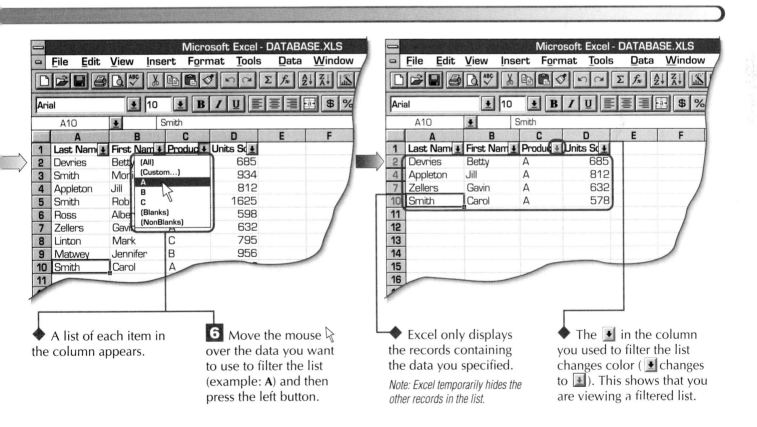

◆ A list of each item in the column appears.

6 Move the mouse ⌖ over the data you want to use to filter the list (example: **A**) and then press the left button.

◆ Excel only displays the records containing the data you specified.

Note: Excel temporarily hides the other records in the list.

◆ The ⬇ in the column you used to filter the list changes color (⬇ changes to ⬇). This shows that you are viewing a filtered list.

FILTER A LIST

When filtering data in a list, you can use operators to perform a more specific search.

FILTER A LIST (USING OPERATORS)

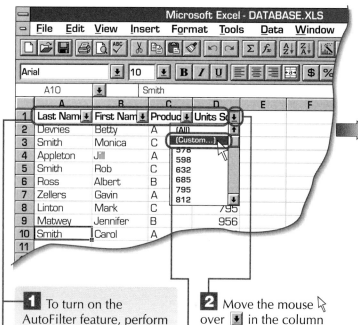

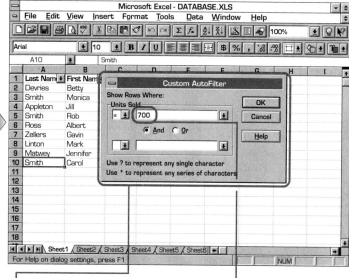

1 To turn on the AutoFilter feature, perform steps **1** to **4** on page 216.

◆ When the AutoFilter feature is on, ⬇ appears beside each field name in your list.

2 Move the mouse ⬚ over ⬇ in the column you want to use to filter the list (example: **Units Sold**) and then press the left button.

3 Move the mouse ⬚ over (**Custom...**) and then press the left button.

◆ The **Custom AutoFilter** dialog box appears.

Note: In this example, Excel will display all records with a value less than 700 (<700).

4 Type the data you want to use to filter the list (example: **700**).

Change Your Screen Display	Using Multiple Worksheets	Using Multiple Workbooks	Charting Data	Enhance a Chart	Drawing Objects	Manage Data in a List

OPERATORS

= finds all records that match

> finds all records that are higher

< finds all records that are lower

>= finds all records that match or are higher

<= finds all records that match or are lower

<> finds all records that do not match

Note: 1 is lower than 2, A is lower than B.

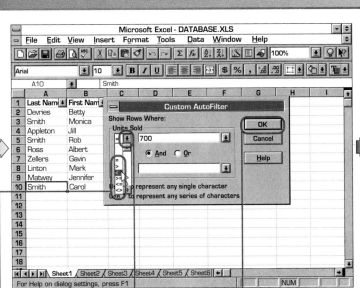

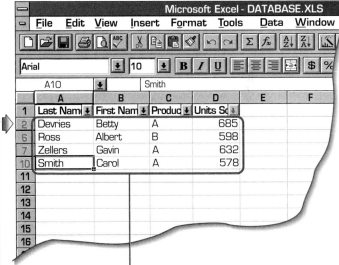

5 To select an operator, move the mouse ⬚ over ⬇ and then press the left button.

6 Move the mouse ⬚ over the operator you want to use (example: <) and then press the left button.

7 Move the mouse ⬚ over **OK** and then press the left button.

◆ The list only displays the records that match the data you specified.

*Note: To unfilter a list, perform steps **2** to **4** on page 216.*

219

SORT DATA

You can use the Sort feature to quickly change the order of the records in your list.

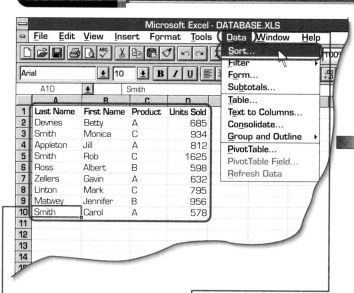

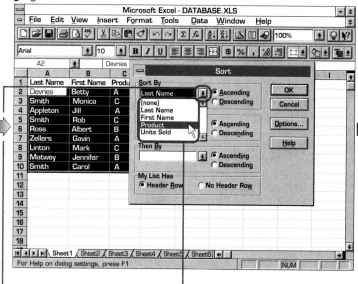

In this example, Excel will sort the products alphabetically.

1 Move the mouse ⊹ over any cell in the list and then press the left button.

2 Move the mouse ⇧ over **Data** and then press the left button.

3 Move the mouse ⇧ over **Sort** and then press the left button.

◆ The **Sort** dialog box appears.

4 To select the category you want to sort, move the mouse ⇧ over ⬇ under **Sort By** and then press the left button.

◆ A list of field names appears.

5 Move the mouse ⇧ over the field name you want to sort (example: **Product**) and then press the left button.

220

WORKING WITH EXCEL

| Change Your Screen Display | Using Multiple Worksheets | Using Multiple Workbooks | Charting Data | Enhance a Chart | Drawing Objects | Manage Data in a List |

- Introduction
- Create a List
- Find Data in a List
- Filter a List
- **Sort Data**
- Add Subtotals to a List
- Hide or Display Subtotaled Data

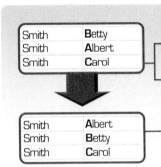

SECONDARY SORTS

◆ In this example, the records are alphabetically sorted by last name.

◆ If a last name appears more than once in your list (example: **Smith**), you can perform a secondary sort.

◆ A **secondary sort** by first name arranges the first names in alphabetical order.

To perform a secondary sort:

1 To select the first category you want to sort, perform steps **1** to **6** below.

2 To select the second category you want to sort, perform steps **4** to **6** below in the first **Then By** area of the **Sort** dialog box.

3 To perform the sort, move the mouse ⬚ over **OK** and then press the left button.

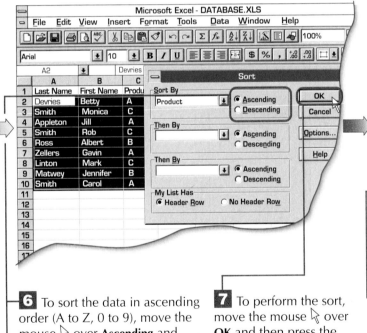

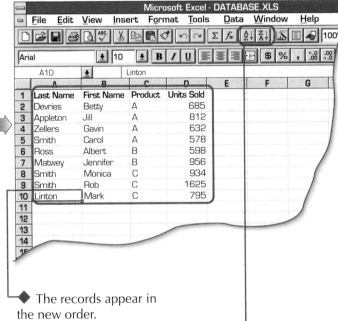

6 To sort the data in ascending order (A to Z, 0 to 9), move the mouse ⬚ over **Ascending** and then press the left button.

◆ To sort the data in descending order (Z to A, 9 to 0), move the mouse ⬚ over **Descending** and then press the left button.

7 To perform the sort, move the mouse ⬚ over **OK** and then press the left button.

◆ The records appear in the new order.

To quickly sort your data:

1 Move the mouse ➕ over any cell in the column you want to sort and then press the left button.

2 Move the mouse ⬚ over one of the following options and then press the left button.

📊↓ Sorts the data in ascending order.

📊↓ Sorts the data in descending order.

ADD SUBTOTALS TO A LIST

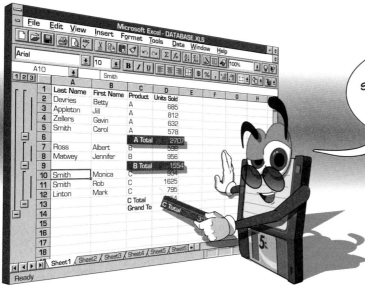

You can quickly summarize data by adding subtotals to your list.

ADD SUBTOTALS TO A LIST

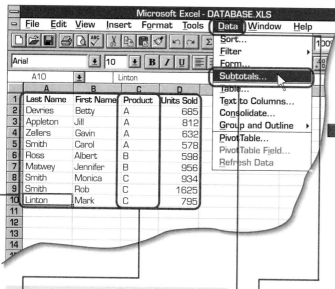

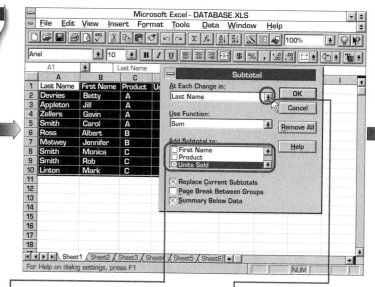

1 To display a total for each item in a column (example: **Product A, B and C**), you must first sort the column. This places all matching items together.

Note: To sort data, refer to page 220.

2 Move the mouse ⬦ over any cell in the list and then press the left button.

3 Move the mouse ⬦ over **Data** and then press the left button.

4 Move the mouse ⬦ over **Subtotals** and then press the left button.

◆ The **Subtotal** dialog box appears.

5 An x must appear in the box beside the category you want to subtotal. To display an x, move the mouse ⬦ over the category and then press the left button.

6 Move the mouse ⬦ over ⬇ in the **At Each Change in**: box and then press the left button.

222

Tip

The Subtotal feature lets you quickly add data in a list.

You can also use this feature to calculate the average, minimum or maximum values in each category.

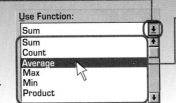

1 In the **Subtotal** dialog box, move the mouse ⬉ over ⬇ in the **Use Function:** box and then press the left button.

2 Move the mouse ⬉ over the option you want to use and then press the left button.

Note: To add subtotals to a list, use the **Sum** option.

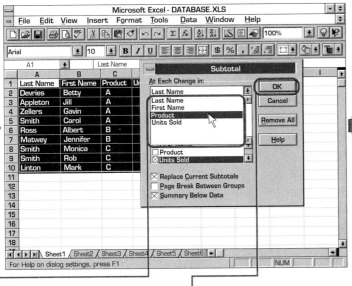

◆ A list of field names appears.

7 A subtotal will appear each time data in a field changes. To select the field name, move the mouse ⬉ over the name (example: **Product**) and then press the left button.

8 Move the mouse ⬉ over **OK** and then press the left button.

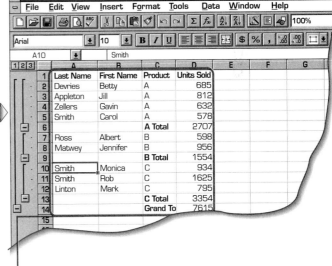

◆ Your list displays subtotals and a grand total.

Note: To remove subtotals, refer to the top of page 225.

HIDE OR DISPLAY SUBTOTALED DATA

After you add subtotals, you can hide or display different levels of data in your list.

CLICK

HIDE OR DISPLAY SUBTOTALED DATA

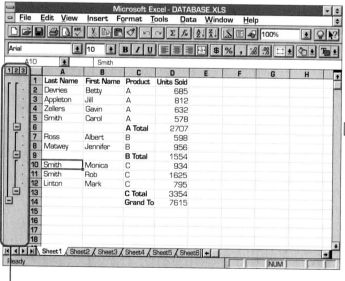

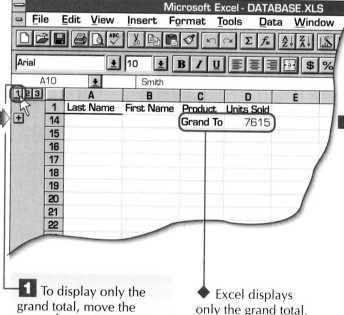

◆ A subtotaled list displays symbols on the left side of the screen.

Note: To add subtotals to a list, refer to page 222.

1 To display only the grand total, move the mouse ⬚ over **1** and then press the left button.

◆ Excel displays only the grand total.

REMOVE SUBTOTALS

1 Move the mouse ➕ over any cell in the list and then press the left button.

2 Move the mouse ⌖ over **Data** and then press the left button.

3 Move the mouse ⌖ over **Subtotals** and then press the left button.

4 Move the mouse ⌖ over **Remove All** and then press the left button.

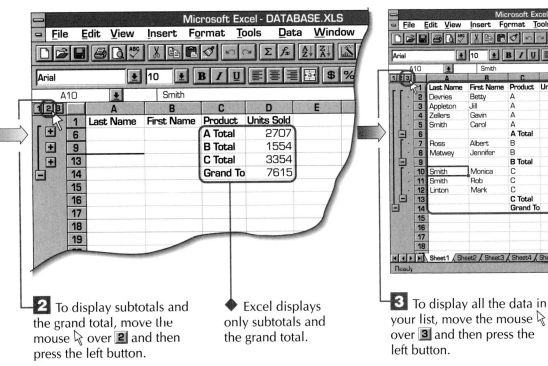

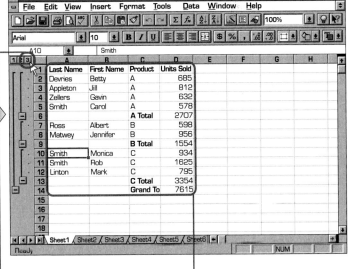

2 To display subtotals and the grand total, move the mouse ⌖ over **2** and then press the left button.

◆ Excel displays only subtotals and the grand total.

3 To display all the data in your list, move the mouse ⌖ over **3** and then press the left button.

◆ Excel displays all of your data with subtotals and the grand total.

INDEX